If the Church Were Christian

Rediscovering the Values of Jesus

PHILIP GULLEY

HarperOne
An Imprint of HarperCollinsPublishers

HarperOne

HarperCollins books may be purchased for educational, business, or sales promotional use. For information please write: Special Markets Department, HarperCollins Publishers, 10 East 53rd Street, New York, NY 10022.

HarperCollins website: http://www.harpercollins.com
HarperCollins®, 👑 ®, and HarperOne™
are trademarks of HarperCollins Publishers

FIRST HARPERCOLLINS PAPERBACK EDITION PUBLISHED IN 2011
Designed by Level C

Library of Congress Cataloging-in-Publication Data
Gulley, Philip.
If the church were Christian : rediscovering the values of Jesus / by Philip Gulley.
— 1st ed.
p. cm.
ISBN 978–0–06–169877–4
1. Church—Biblical teaching. 2. Jesus Christ—Teachings. 3. Jesus Christ—Example. I. Title.
BS2417.C53G85 2010
261'.1—dc22
2009019819

11 12 13 14 15 BV 10 9 8 7 6 5 4 3 2

This book is dedicated to the memory of my maternal
grandmother, Norma Quinett, who first taught me
one could be both faithful and loving

Contents

Acknowledgments

My previous two theological books—*If Grace Is True* and *If God Is Love*—were written with Jim Mulholland, a fellow Quaker. Because of other commitments and shifting life priorities, Jim was unable to partner with me on this book. I felt his absence every day in the writing of this book. His keen mind and ability to reduce complex matters to an accessible form were blessings to me. I look forward to the day we can cowrite again.

In order to guard the anonymity of persons, I have often changed names, genders, and settings. As the occasional target of religious watchdogs, I am reluctant to reveal the names of persons whose sense of grace compelled them to operate outside the creeds and rules, lest they become targets too.

Most of these chapters had their genesis in messages I gave in a variety of churches, retreat centers, and colleges around the country, including my own faith community, Fairfield Friends Meeting, near Indianapolis. Everyone should be privileged to be in community with such fine people.

Every book I've written was only possible because others worked alongside me. I am especially indebted to Steve Hanselman, Steve Green, Byron Williamson, and the good people of HarperOne who work so creatively on my behalf—Mark Tauber, Mickey Maudlin, Cynthia DiTiberio, Laina Adler, Julie Burton, Terri Leonard, Jim Warner, and Sam Barry.

My thanks to Stacey Denny, who makes me appear more organized than I am. She is a rare blend of grace and competence, and I am grateful for her assistance. If you've appreciated the GraceTalks Web site, PhilipGulley.org, you have Stacey Denny to thank.

I am also thankful for the churches, retreat centers, and colleges who endured the earliest forms of this book. Their thoughtful responses sharpened my thinking and elevated my spirit.

As always, I am indebted to my wife, Joan, and two sons, Spencer and Sam, who for many years have tolerated my theological forays with good humor.

If you wish to write me, please do so through my Web site, PhilipGulley.org. Unfortunately, I can't respond to every handwritten letter, especially those containing multiple Bible verses pointing out my theological inadequacies. I do make an effort to answer every e-mail, and that remains the best way to reach me.

One closing note: If, after reading this book, you have the impression I represent the Christianity I describe, you would be mistaken. Each of us has a dream; living up to the principles articulated in this book is mine.

Introduction

When I was seven years old and preparing for my first communion, the teacher explained the illustrious history of our church—our miraculous beginnings, those seasons of peril when God intervened to preserve us, the heroic figures who led our church through the wilderness, the glorious conviction that our church alone had remained faithful to Jesus's vision. Naturally, I was grateful I'd been born into the one true church.[1]

While I was delighted at my good fortune, I worried about my father's family, who generations before had allied themselves with an apostate movement. We were regularly encouraged to pray for those who belonged to "lesser" churches. Jesus spoke of such people, those who said "Lord, Lord," but wouldn't enter the kingdom of heaven. He was talking, I was certain, about my relatives.

When I was a teenager, I was discussing religion with a friend who belonged to another denomination. I was surprised to discover that his church had the same vaunted history as mine. They, too, were uniquely chosen and blessed by God. They, too, traced their lineage to Jesus. They, too, were obedient to God's Word. They, too, remained uniquely pure, untainted by the world. They, too, were praying—but for me.

Initially, I found this unsettling. I wasn't sure which one of us was deceived. Given the nature of exclusive claims, one of us had to be wrong. My friend's certainty seemed so complete, it caused me to doubt mine. I began to suspect I'd been misled, and when he urged me to visit his church, I went. Within a year, I'd joined his Quaker meeting, convinced I'd discovered the real thing.

In my adult years, I began to wonder if the language of ecclesiastical purity, such as "the One True Church" and "the Reformed Church," was based on a faulty assumption—that we can actually know what Jesus intended the church to be. Whether our arguments for spiritual supremacy relied on an unbroken chain of apostolic succession, a literal reading of an inerrant Bible, or an insight gained in a moment of spiritual enlightenment, we all claimed to know the heart and mind of Jesus and his hope for the church, despite little evidence that Jesus even gave the church much thought. Most of what we assert about the church is based on fragmentary hints from Jesus and two thousand years of tradition.

Several years ago I visited a museum and saw the skeleton of a dinosaur. As I read the plaque, I learned only a handful of the bones were original, that the remainder had been fabricated based on a paleontologist's extrapolation from the authentic bones. In many ways, this is similar to what the church has done. There are only two passages in one gospel (Matthew 16:18 and 18:17) where Jesus mentions the church, and even those references are dubious. Many scholars suspect the Matthean verses were not original to Jesus but were written back into the text by persons hoping to bolster their theological and ecclesial positions by placing them in the mouth of Jesus. From those two verses, we have built a vast institution based on these "hints" Jesus gave us. But we should never delude ourselves into thinking that today's church sprang directly from the mind and witness of Jesus. All we have is extrapolation, a few bones upon which have been erected a larger organism.

If Jesus intended to create the church, he did a questionable job. He left no clear directions about its structure or purpose. The apostle Paul and others would later do that, but Jesus didn't. Jesus did no fund-raising. In fact, he seemed unconcerned about financial development, telling his disciples to take no money for their ministry. If the disciples were his first board of directors, he chose poorly. In their first major decision, replacing Judas, they shunned standard business practices and drew lots.

Jesus did none of the things essential to forming a viable institution. Some may argue that Jesus wasn't negligent, that he was simply confident in the Holy Spirit's ability to guide and grow the fledgling church. But Jesus's cautionary, even hostile, language about religious institutions makes such a claim doubtful, if not incredible. A fair reading of the earliest gospels offers scant evidence that Jesus intended to start a new religion.

Though a convincing argument could be made that Jesus didn't found the church, it seems unlikely that present-day Christians will disband their congregations. For many of us, it's difficult to imagine a world without the church. Even if Jesus didn't intend to start the church, it will likely endure in one form or another. But if the church claims Jesus as its founder, it should at least share his values. The question for Christians is whether the church reflects the priorities of Jesus.

This question has divided the church again and again. There are roughly 39,000 Christian denominations, each of which has a slightly different take on the priorities of Jesus.[2] All denominations, whether liberal or conservative, share the conviction that they most faithfully follow Jesus. They earnestly believe Jesus imagined the church as looking just like them. When I became a Quaker, I sincerely believed Jesus had been raised in an early version of a Quaker meetinghouse.

It seems arrogant for any of us to suggest that we alone have most accurately discerned the true intentions of Jesus. This is always the great temptation. After I wrote my books on universal salvation,[3] I was often approached by persons urging me to start a new denomination. They believed my opinion of a specific theological doctrine was an adequate foundation for a new institution. I declined their invitations for three reasons: I found community with my own church satisfying; I had no confidence in my ability to create a pure Christianity after thirty-nine thousand denominations had tried and failed; and I feared that being a key figure in a new movement would expand my head and shrink my heart.

In addition to the growing diversity of the Christian faith, there has been an explosion of knowledge in the past hundred years about the Bible and its formation. While this has broadened our understanding of Jesus and his culture, it has also cast doubt on what the church had always assumed were the authentic sayings and activities of Jesus. The era of uncritical acceptance of Jesus stories is past and with it the church's claim to a divinely ordained status.

Gone also is the clear blueprint for Christian conduct we assumed Matthew, Mark, Luke, and John offered. The gospel accounts, written some thirty to sixty years after the death of Jesus, are the early church's words about Jesus, not necessarily the actual words of Jesus. So to even say "Jesus said this" or "Jesus said that" is to make an assumption that might not be true.

Nevertheless, the story of Jesus is a compelling one and still has the power to shape, form, and transform our lives. We can just no longer assume there is universal agreement on what that story means, if ever we could. Nor can we assume that the gospel versions of the Jesus story are historically accurate. The lessons might well be existentially true—that is, they possess a spiritual richness and value—but to claim they are historically accurate is likely an overstatement and a misunderstanding of their genre and purpose.

All of these developments—the staggering number of denominations, the rise of biblical criticism, and the diminishing authority of the church and the Bible—have made it impossible to articulate a universal understanding of what it means to be Christian. This should not deter us from offering our particular understanding of Christianity, so long as we bear in mind we are speaking from our own experience and our experience is always limited.

Though beliefs within Christendom vary, and the chance for universal consensus is slim, we still must think creatively about what it means to be Christian and what we mean when we say the church is Christian, even though that description will grow outdated. For it is also clear that what it means to be Christian has changed dramatically over the centuries and will continue to change. The "old-time religion" of which some still sing is a relatively new-time religion, not "good enough for the Hebrew children," not even recognizable to them.

Even as the understanding of what it means to be Christian has shifted, so has the word itself. We speak of "doing our Christian duty" and by that mean doing what we believe to be virtuous and good, apart from any specific belief about Jesus. Whatever the word *Christianity* might have meant at one time, it now means—to many, many people—being nice.

A woman once phoned, asking if I could officiate at her wedding. Some pastors have strict theological criteria about whom they will marry. While I don't, before I could even explain my protocol, the woman hastened to inform me she was Christian.

"Oh, what church do you attend?" I asked.

"I've never really gone to church," she said.

If I had been defining Christianity strictly by one's participation in a Christian community, she would not have been Christian. But I hadn't, so our conversation continued.

"Did you mean to say that Jesus is your Savior?" I asked.

"I don't think so," she said.

"What do you mean, then, when you say you're a Christian?" I asked, my curiosity growing.

"I guess what I meant is that my grandmother goes to church and I grew up in America," she said.

So Christianity was something one inherited by virtue of his or her lineage or nationality.

I didn't challenge her definition; I simply remembered it and since then have heard it echoed by others. The criteria for Christian faith now seems to be this: if I say I am a Christian, I am.

While those who value theological clarity might bristle at such loose terms, the alternative would have us examining one another closely, judging who among us is fit to bear that name, attempting to construct a definition suitable to all, which is both undesirable and impossible.

All of this is to say that the Christian faith I am about to articulate might well satisfy only a church of one. My faith is informed by my experience as a Roman Catholic and a Quaker, by my twenty-five years in pastoral ministry, by the many diverse people I have encountered in my life, and by my growing conviction that Christianity is less a codified doctrine or creed and more an approach to life that emphasizes grace, is always on the side of human dignity, is always devoted to our spiritual growth and moral evolution, and is always committed to the ongoing search for truth, even if that search leads us away from institutional Christianity.

If my hope in this book is the rediscovery of the values of Jesus, it seems odd to suggest the church might not be the vehicle for that regeneration. But if history has taught us anything, it is that renewal blossoms in the most unlikely places, perhaps even in the church. If you've ever been mystified by the activities of some churches, left to wonder what in the world they had to do with the ethic of Jesus, consider this book an invitation to appraise our current priorities and whether they honor the Christian values we claim to cherish.

Such introspection is not always welcomed by the church. For the past several years, there has been a sustained effort to rescind my credentials as a pastor in the Religious Society of Friends. While these efforts have at times been a distraction, they have served to confirm my hunch that any religion whose goal is the exclusion of others is bound to fail, if only because it cannot ignite our imaginations and sustain our spirits.

With these qualifications, and with the ready admission of my own inconsistency in living out these ideals, I offer my thoughts on what the church might look like if it were Christian.

1. The word *church* has sometimes been capitalized when referring to the universal church—the Church. It conveys a sense of privilege and entitlement this Quaker increasingly rejects. In the interests of ecclesial modesty, I have elected not to do that in this book, believing it confers a status not always merited. In my mind, such grammatical tributes should be earned, not demanded.

2. According to the Gordon-Conwell Theological Seminary's "Status of Global Mission, 2008" report, there are now over 39,000 Christian denominations in the world.

3. *If Grace Is True* and *If God Is Love*, both published by HarperOne and co-written with James Mulholland.

If the Church Were Christian . . .

Jesus Would Be a Model for Living
Rather Than an Object of Worship

I was born into a mixed marriage. My father hailed from Baptists, and my mother from Roman Catholics. My father was religiously indifferent and ceded the spiritual ground to my mother, who took me and my siblings to Mass each Sunday morning in the small town where we lived. The building was a modest one, intended as a temporary structure until the congregation had grown sufficiently to erect a more suitable building. Unfortunately, our priests were near retirement, depleted of physical and spiritual energy, and unable to expand the church's population. For as long as I attended there, the building where we gathered to worship was small and plain, with one exception—behind the altar hung a magnificent figure of Jesus nailed to a cross.

The statue was so realistic as to be frightening. Nails protruded from Jesus's wrists and ankles, blood mingled down in a grisly red, his body striped with angry lashes. The figure loomed above the priest, inescapable. It had to be gazed upon. Without my mother telling me so, I deduced this Jesus was to be revered. Had the statue been placed anywhere else, had it been avoidable, I do not think it would have captured my attention to the extent it did. But its being placed behind the altar, squarely in the center of the worshippers' attentions, forced me to gaze upon it, brought it sharply into focus, and required a response. It was clear from the priest's words and from the hymns we sang and prayers we offered that the hoped-for response was veneration. This Jesus was to be worshipped. Further, the quality and sincerity of my worship would determine my future, whether I would enjoy an eternal life of joy and bliss with Jesus, or an eternity of suffering and sorrow without him.

Several assertions were made about Jesus, all of which were offered as proof of his divine status, fundamentally different from us, therefore meriting our worship. These included his divine origins, his ability to perform miracles, and his sinless nature.

Long before I understood human reproduction, I was told Jesus was born of a virgin. Because I lacked scientific knowledge and trusted the persons telling me this, I believed it was true. It would be many years before I understood the irrationality of such a claim, and even more years before I mustered the courage to question it. Meanwhile, it served to elevate Jesus in my eyes, which was its intended purpose. I would later learn that stories of virginal origins were not unique to Jesus. Ancient mythologies were rife with similar assertions about their central figures, all of which had the effect of raising those persons above other mortals. In Christianity, the myth of the virgin birth not only served to exalt Jesus, it reinforced an emerging trend within the movement that relegated women to an inferior role. In a culture that viewed sexual behavior as sinful, and women as the cause of humanity's fall, it isn't surprising the church would diminish Mary's biological role in the birth of Jesus. Rather than a co-creator of Jesus, Mary became the pure vessel through which God's unblemished Son was delivered, requiring no genetic or sexual contribution on her part, leaving her virginity (and reputation) intact.

Another assertion about Jesus that set him apart from humanity was his capacity for manipulating nature, persons, and events to demonstrate God's power and presence. To read the Gospels is to encounter the one who stilled storms, raised the dead, passed ghostlike through hostile mobs, healed the blind, restored the lame, walked on water, and on at least two occasions generated enough food to feed thousands of people with a handful of loaves and fishes. But Jesus was not the only biblical figure to whom miracles were attributed. Moses turned the waters of Egypt to blood, Joshua commanded the sun to stand still, Elijah caused water-saturated wood to spontaneously combust, and Peter healed a man lame from birth. Even persons who worshipped false gods were able to conjure up the occasional miracle.

I'm often asked whether I believe the miracles of Jesus actually occurred. At one time, I answered positively, certain the events of the Bible had transpired just as they were written. I no longer make that claim. I now interpret those activities as pre-Enlightenment affirmations of the transforming presence of Jesus. That is, ancient people, moved by their encounters with Jesus, sought to convey their appreciation for him in the only language they knew—miracle stories, parables, and wisdom sayings. One consequence of that language was to elevate the stature of Jesus. While I question the divinity of Jesus as it has been traditionally taught, I do not question his apparent gift of directing persons to God in such a commanding and compelling manner that lives and circumstances were changed, often dramatically so. I have experienced such change myself and witnessed it in others.

In addition to his extraordinary origins and miraculous activities, I was also taught that Jesus was without sin. The moral perfection of Jesus was the keystone of Christian orthodoxy, and to doubt it was to risk damnation. While our access to Jesus's words about himself are limited, it is important to note he never made such a claim for himself. If he did, the writers of the Gospels didn't feel inclined to record and convey what would eventually become a major Christian doctrine.

Was Jesus sinless? The classic definition of sin is to knowingly and willfully choose to do evil. Central to that understanding is one's mental, spiritual, and emotional capacity to make appropriate moral decisions. Were a three-year-old to kill someone, we would rightly call it evil, in that it thwarted the hope and purpose of God. But we would not call it a sin, since the child lacked the capacity to make the intentional choice to do evil. This is why we don't imprison toddlers, and limit the culpability of persons encumbered by a mental disability. Sin has to do with intentionality and one's ability to choose between good and evil. Whether or not Jesus was sinless remains unknown to me and, quite honestly, of little importance. Were I to learn that at the age of fifteen Jesus willfully disobeyed his parents or experienced adolescent feelings of sexual longing, my respect for his life and witness would not be diminished. (The moral purity of Jesus was key to the church's understanding and teaching that Jesus was the unblemished sacrifice made on our behalf to save us from God's wrath and judgment. When one rejects that view of God, Jesus's moral purity is no longer imperative.)[1]

So from an early age I was taught that Jesus's divine origins, miracle-working power, and moral perfection confirmed his uniqueness and merited our adoration. In my early years this made sense to me, and my life in the church consisted of praising and worshipping Jesus as the divine Son of God. All the while, the church told me this was both appropriate and necessary. Given the church's sacrifice-centered theology, this held a certain logic, and I didn't question it.

When I left the Roman Catholic Church as a teenager, I began visiting other churches and discovered these perceptions of Jesus transcended denominational boundaries. Their worship and theology were similarly Jesus focused. Nowhere was this more obvious than in the congregational songs. By then, praise music had made its way into the churches. Hymnals gathered dust, while lyrics were displayed on a screen behind the pulpit. These praise songs were simple, often repeating the same phrase over and over, usually having to do with the adoration of Jesus. I sung these songs with much passion, their effect on me almost hypnotic, which was perhaps their intended result.

As my interest in Christianity grew, I began reading the Bible and enrolled in college to study theology and engage religious matters more deeply. I became enamored with the life story of Jesus. His courage in the face of rigid religion, his compassion for the outcast, his insight into human nature, and his fresh way of articulating the priorities of God garnered both my attention and admiration.

But the more I learned about the historical Jesus and the Jewish setting in which he lived, the more I wondered how he would have felt about his promotion to divine status and subsequent elevation as an object of worship. Would he have welcomed such veneration as his due? Or, as a monotheistic Jew, would he have interpreted such reverence as idolatrous? Of course, it is intellectually risky to read someone's mind two thousand years after his or her death. But this has not kept us from claiming to know the mind of Jesus, even about matters with which he couldn't have been familiar, such as evolution, abortion, the American political system, and other topics. So even as I imagine how Jesus might have felt about his promotion to divine status, I am well aware I might be mistaken. But I risk the discussion because I believe the church's worship of Jesus is something he would not have favored. Further, this tendency has had profound consequences, not all of them beneficial.

One consequence has been our tendency to value right thinking above right acting. When I first indicated my interest in becoming a pastor, a church invited me to work with their youth. Why they entrusted their most vulnerable members to my inexperienced oversight was a mystery, but this happens often in churches, occasionally with good results. The church was located in a solidly middle-class area, which hampered my efforts to introduce the children to human need and heighten their sense of social responsibility. So I arranged to transport the youth to the inner city of Indianapolis to help renovate a homeless shelter. My ministry was overseen by a board of elders, most of whom approved this undertaking, except for one man who sat with his arms folded, clearly unimpressed with my proposal. After the meeting he took me aside and objected to the project.

"If those people would just work, they wouldn't be in that place," he said. "We ought not coddle them. Why are you doing this?"

I pointed out that the residents of the shelter were victims of spousal and child abuse and came there seeking safety. "These aren't lazy people. They've had bad luck. We're Christians, and I think we should help them."

"What's being a Christian got to do with it?" he asked.

I chuckled, thinking he was joking, then realized he wasn't, that in his mind being Christian had little to do with acts of compassion. During my time at that church, I got to know the man better and observed that while his enthusiasm for orthodoxy was great, he had little passion for ministry. He believed all the "right" things about Jesus and could give his intellectual assent to the tenets of traditional Christianity. If tests had been given to measure one's orthodoxy, he would have been a star student. But for some reason this had never translated into a zeal for service. For him, being a Christian had everything to do with worshipping Jesus and little to do with following his example.

I hasten to add that while I have met other people like him, I have known many others who take right belief and right action seriously, whose appreciation for orthodoxy is matched by their mercy and compassion. But it's also clear that for some people in the church, belief is not only everything—it is the only thing. Indeed, I have noticed many Christians refer to themselves as "believers," as if Christianity is primarily about believing.

But what if Jesus didn't want people to believe certain tenets about him, so much as take seriously the kingdom ethos he promoted? Was the goal of Jesus to convince people he was divine? Did he want to establish a new religion whose chief purpose was his adoration? Though that is precisely what has happened, I doubt it is what Jesus had in mind.

There are other books that better describe how Jesus became God, a process that unfolded over hundreds of years, involving political manipulation, violence, and power grabs.[2] Many in the contemporary church assume Jesus's identity and nature were immediately apparent, universally agreed upon, and clearly stated, but such is not the case. The issue of Jesus's nature absorbed much of the church's attention for nearly three hundred years, culminating in the Arian controversy and the First Council of Nicea in 325 CE when the church's bishops gathered to discern, among other things, the nature of Jesus. Inevitably, when any institution has determined the truth, those reluctant to embrace it are seen as a threat and are often silenced, excommunicated, or even killed. Looming over this council was the towering presence of the emperor Constantine, who wished to unify (and exploit) the church for his own political purposes. Not surprisingly, the bishops voted to declare Jesus God. One might question the accuracy of any "truth" arrived at by voting, whose desired outcome is expressed by a powerful government. But questioning such matters is seldom appreciated, and those who encourage the church to consider other alternatives discover their popularity fading.

Several years ago, I was interviewed by a man writing an article for a magazine. While the interviewer was not a theologian, he was curious about spiritual matters and asked what I thought about Jesus, specifically about his divinity. I expressed doubts about his divinity, at least in the way the church has typically defined it, and said, by way of explanation, "He [Jesus] was a monotheistic Jew who did not see himself as divine. He saw himself as a rabbi, probably a prophet." I chose my words carefully, knowing they would be quoted. Wanting to affirm my deep appreciation for the life and witness of Jesus, I added, "But I certainly understand the personality of God through the person of Jesus. That is, I believe God's priorities were also Jesus' priorities, and those priorities were to care for the poor and the marginalized."[3]

Within a short time, calls demanding the rescinding of my recording (ordination) were circulating through our yearly meeting (an organization of local Quaker meetings). Again and again, the same charge was voiced—questioning the divinity of Jesus was unacceptable. Even in a denomination as tolerant as the Quakers, a pastor was not allowed to express reservations about a matter that had confounded thoughtful and sincere Christians for thousands of years. For the next several years, I was summoned before committees, asked to affirm doctrines in a denomination that expressly rejected creedalism, and, when I declined to do so, was urged to leave ministry and Quakerism. I had become a Quaker precisely because of its theological and intellectual freedom, only to discover the limits of that freedom. Fortunately, more rational voices carried the day, but not before the chill winds of wrath and fear had done their damage.

If I use any divine language in regard to Jesus, I tend to use the language of my Quaker tradition, which talks about "that of God in all people." This understanding allows me to celebrate God's presence in Jesus, while affirming that same divine reality in others. Perhaps Jesus lived more fully in this presence than most, but within everyone there exists the potential to live as he did. I realize this distinction isn't sufficient for many Christians, that they will insist on the unique divinity of Jesus, but this Christian believes the same God who so enlivened Jesus also enlivens others. Unfortunately, such hopes, when voiced aloud, are often silenced or scorned.

This is where we are today—before any substantive discussion about Jesus can occur, his divine status as the second person of the Trinity must be acknowledged, even if Jesus never made such a claim for himself and might even have been offended by it.[4]

I argue against the deification of Jesus because of my admiration for him. I believe his promotion to divine statue contradicts the Jewish faith of Jesus and ultimately encourages behavior inconsistent with the ethic of Jesus. It has made the church overly proud and prone to asserting itself as the only path to God. In questioning this claim, my wish is not to diminish the life of Jesus, but to honor it as fully as I can by asking whether his elevation to divinity is something he would have wanted. One telling clue to Jesus's self-awareness can be found in the tenth chapter of the gospel of Mark when Jesus was approached by a man who called him "Good Teacher" (v. 17). Jesus's response was immediate and startling, "Why do you call me good? No one is good but God alone" (v. 18). I have heard some say Jesus was, in a clever way, offering the man the opportunity to affirm his divinity, but that is not what happened. Jesus simply directed the man to a style of living he believed would honor the priorities of God. Clearly, Jesus was a man who did not comfortably accept affirmations of divinity as his due.

I also raise the question of divinity as a matter of integrity, living as we do in an era when many thoughtful Christians value the priorities of Jesus but reject the creeds and legends that have built up around him. The question for today's church isn't whether or not Jesus was divine. We should be asking ourselves what it meant when earlier Christians made that claim, then find a way to affirm the value of Jesus in language that doesn't require the suspension of reason, science, and grace.

Lest you consider such a matter trivial, consider for a moment the damage done by theological exclusivity. When any religion claims a unique divine status for its founder, the next inevitable step is exclusion. "Our religion is the true path to God! All other religions are false." Tolerance, acceptance, and mutual respect fall by the way. Justifications are made not only to treat others poorly, but sometimes even to kill them. One can examine almost any conflict in our world today and find behind it the poison of exclusive religion, one group murdering another in the name of their God. Our world can ill afford the high cost of divine privilege that elevates some and denigrates others. The time has come for a new language, a language that honors Jesus, though not at the expense of his own self-understanding and our own need to live in peace.

What would it mean if Jesus were a model for living rather than an object of worship?

At the age of eighteen, when my interest in Christianity was rekindled, I attended a friend's church. Accustomed to the more subdued worship style of Catholics and Quakers, I was intrigued by my friend's pastor, who was more casual and outgoing. While his tone was conversational, his message was dead serious—there were doctrines one had to believe to enjoy right relationship with God. Specifically, I was asked to believe Jesus was God, that I was sinful, that the divine Jesus had died on my behalf to save me from God's judgment, and by believing those things, I would go to heaven when I died. The pastor then offered the congregants an opportunity to come forward and publicly affirm the theology he'd just shared. I was young, and frightened, so I went forward.

Though I no longer embrace that theology, the experience of going forward ignited in me a desire to learn more, so I don't regret it. What I do regret is believing for a number of years that the sole value of Jesus rested in his ability to usher me into heaven. This was reinforced by my friend's preacher, who downplayed any other value Jesus might have offered, especially the power of Jesus's good example.

"Some people will tell you Jesus is only an example for how we should live," he said. "But anyone can be an example."

Thirty years have passed since I heard that sermon, and one thing I've learned is the difficulty of being a good example. I've known many people who've exemplified one or two virtues, but I've known very few persons who've consistently embodied the qualities and values we associate with godly virtue. Moreover, I have witnessed the damage done—when appropriate models were lacking—to children whose parents failed to provide a loving example and to teens whose friends and family were unable to serve as helpful models for living. I have heard teachers, judges, and social workers lament the scarcity of good examples in the lives of children they've encountered.

I have failed to be an appropriate model for Christian conduct many times. At significant points, when I should have led by example, I failed to embody the very principles I publicly affirm. I have been intolerant, greedy, slothful, and even dishonest. Were someone to say I was an example for how others should live, I would be flattered but would know their assessment was inaccurate. To say Jesus is "only an example," as if that were a small thing, underestimates not only the profound difficulty of serving such a role, but also discounts its rarity.

I have heard this disparagement of example by many Christians, most often by those who've emphasized orthodoxy over conduct. Though we can't know with certainty Jesus's self-understanding, I suspect his chief hope was to embody the values of God. Indeed, if someone had accused him of being "only an example," he would have likely replied, "What is wrong with that? Shouldn't we all be?"

Consider this: Jesus offered no new revelation from God. Everything he said and did grew out of his Jewish faith. As in all religions, there were those in Judaism who'd forgotten and forsaken its principles. What first-century Judaism needed wasn't a new revelation, but the reminder of a previous one. The prophets preceding Jesus had described well the priorities of God—mercy, forgiveness, hospitality, and compassion. Jesus exemplified those virtues, expanded their meaning for his generation, and through the power of his good example, urged others to not only imitate his works, but to exceed them.

What Jesus wasn't about was his own glorification and elevation. Rather, he argued for humility, modesty, and putting others before self. This was not a man claiming a special status for himself, but a man committed to faithfully living out the priorities of God's reign and helping others do the same. Being a fitting example was precisely what he was about. Instead of accepting that, the church made Jesus God, interpreting his life in ways he likely didn't intend, convincing itself that his way of living was only possible because he was God, providing humanity an excuse not to be like him.

In my twenty-five years of pastoral ministry, I have heard people say time and again, "I could never be like Jesus." But what I've discovered in the Gospels is the expectation that we could and should be like him.

The Christian gospel ought not be that Jesus was God and we can find life in his death. Our good news is that we can find life in his example—accepting the excluded, healing the sick, strengthening the weak, loving the despised, and challenging the powerful to use their influence redemptively. These objectives do not require divinity, but commitment, compassion, and courage. Jesus accomplished what he did not because of some supernatural power unavailable to the rest of us; he accomplished what he did because of his steadfast dedication to the priorities of God.

Several years ago, a fellow Quaker and friend, Ray Stewart, lay dying in a hospital. He was advanced in years, had suffered a number of health setbacks, was near death, and knew it. But the day we visited, his senses were sharp, his mood good. While Ray had taken his faith seriously, he was not always a friend of orthodoxy and had a habit of distressing more conventional members of our denomination. Because he could be outspoken, some people dismissed him as crotchety, but I found him to be genuine and loving.

While I stood by his bedside, he took my hand and gave me several parting instructions, knowing it would likely be our last opportunity to speak.

"Philip," he said. "If you ever hurt your children, apologize to them. The mark of a man isn't his pride, but his humility."

I nodded my head.

"But don't be a pisswilly," he added.

Ray was always urging me not to be a pisswilly, or an insignificant person.

I had my own parting words for Ray. I promised him I wouldn't be a pisswilly, then said, "Ray, when I grow older, I want to be like you."

He squeezed my hand in silent appreciation. I left shortly afterward, and within a few hours he was dead.

I have reflected on our last conversation many times since Ray's passing. I don't think I could have said anything more meaningful to him. The highest compliment we can ever pay anyone is our desire to be like that person.

Now consider for a moment all the energy the church has devoted these past centuries, getting people to believe theological doctrines about Jesus—sending missionaries around the world, funding and promoting television and radio ministries, going door to door, spending billions of dollars and untold hours urging people to believe certain things, then killing, threatening, or excluding them when they didn't.

What if those sizeable resources had instead been used to be like Jesus, bringing to fruition his hopes and dreams for the world? Of course, I know the church has fed the hungry, clothed the poor, and been the source of great good. I also know we have expended many resources, and created no small amount of ill will, when we have valued orthodoxy over practice. If we in the church were serious about honoring Jesus, conducting ourselves as he did would be our chief concern.

In the chapters ahead, I will be examining in more detail the priorities of Jesus and their implications for his followers. I don't pretend to be a Jesus scholar. There are many others more knowledgeable. My hope is to interpret the life and example of Jesus in a redemptive and relevant way. Each generation must do this with Jesus, lest it be forced into stale beliefs that strain credibility and diminish life. For the joy of Christian faith is not to be found in the rote recitation of dogmas about Jesus, but in modeling his mercy and love, which alone have the power to transform us and our world.

1. Jim Mulholland and I wrote more about this in our book *If Grace Is True*. I bring it up here only to illustrate the manner in which ancient myths continue to influence modern theology.
2. One such book is *When Jesus Became God*, by Richard Rubenstein.
3. Lou Harry, "The Conversation: *IMM* and Pastor Philip Gulley," *Indy Men's Magazine*, December 2005, 57.
4. The theological concept of the Trinity is a perfect example of answering a question with a riddle. For the fun of it, invite a Trinitarian to explain the Trinity to you in language that is comprehensible and rational. I am an advocate of Occam's razor, which generally asserts that the hypothesis that includes the fewest assumptions is the more likely one to be true. The concept of the Trinity abandons reasonable simplicity for inexplicable complexity.

If the Church Were Christian . . .

Affirming Our Potential Would Be More Important Than Condemning Our Brokenness

I was once speaking with the father of several preschoolers. He had phoned our Quaker meeting looking for a church community in which to raise his children.

"My wife and I grew up in the church, but we stopped going," he said. "Now we have children and want them to learn the Bible stories." I assumed by Bible stories appropriate for his children he was referring to the Good Samaritan kind of story and not Joshua's slaughter of the Canaanites kind of story. But something in the tone of his voice made me think he'd be just as happy having his children taught the gruesome stories too, so I added, "The Bible is important to us, so we handle it carefully. Not all of it is helpful, nor is all of it appropriate for children."

His response was immediate. "I grew up on those stories, and I turned out fine."

"I'm glad you did," I said. "Of course, we'd be honored to have your family come visit us. We enjoy visitors." I told him our meeting times, gave him directions to our meetinghouse, and ended the conversation by expressing my hope to meet him and his family the next Sunday.

But I didn't ask him what was on my mind. What I wanted to ask was, "If you have such a high opinion of the church's teachings, why did you leave it?"

In my years of ministry, I have met many people like this man. Exposed to rigid religion as children, they were reminded constantly of their unworthiness, told over and over again of the many ways they had disappointed and angered God. Understandably, they grew resentful toward the church for its maltreatment and left as soon as they could. Some stayed away, but others didn't. Like some who are abused, they found it difficult to sever the relationship with their abuser and returned to the church. Even some who physically left remained emotionally attached.

Eventually they became parents, parenting the way they were raised, as we all tend to do, wanting their children to have a moral foundation, as we all want for our children. So they return to the church. This has been the genius of the church—its knack for convincing us it is the sole provider of morality. Thus, they return to the source of their mistreatment, wanting the church to do for their children what it did for them, since they turned out "fine."

But is it fine when the primary image we have of ourselves is one of worthlessness, brokenness, and failure? Is it all right when the church, which should be uplifting and enriching the human spirit, instead leaves us feeling debased and diminished?

Naturally, there are churches that convey a sense of acceptance, inclusion, and love. But the negative stereotype of church lingers precisely because it is true. Far too many churches, and far too many Christians, elevate God at the expense of humanity. For God to be good, we must be sinners in need of redemption.

Several years ago, a young man who'd recently begun attending our Quaker meeting phoned our house, asking to meet with me. It was late in the evening, but I could sense he was deeply anxious and agreed to drive to the meetinghouse to listen to his concern. On the way over, I wondered what had caused his angst—a death in his family, separation from his girlfriend, the loss of a job, or financial difficulties.

He was waiting for me at the meetinghouse, and we entered and sat side by side on a pew. I sat quietly, waiting for him to speak. His head was bowed, his eyes red.

"I am a disappointment to God," he said.

I didn't say anything, sensing he wanted to reveal something more. "God must be so angry with me." He began to cry.

"Why do you think God is angry with you?" I asked.

He rocked back and forth in the pew, clearly distraught. "I've dishonored God with my language."

His "sin," it turns out, was cussing while out with friends.

He went on to explain the religious environment of his childhood. It was a story I'd heard countless times—well-intentioned parents exposing their children to a spiritually lethal environment, hoping to instill some sense of moral responsibility, instead burdening them with such shame that even the slightest lapse was a cause for crushing guilt.

I have often wondered if some forms of religion couldn't more accurately be classified as a mental illness, given their power to distort the human mind and spirit. Were one determined to damage someone's life, I could imagine few things more destructive than regular exposure to some churches. Guilt is their weapon of choice. Guilt for being born into sin. Guilt for experiencing unavoidable human passions. Guilt for not believing with sufficient zeal. Guilt for questioning settled beliefs. Guilt for doubting. Guilt for minor lapses in proper conduct. Guilt for not spreading the church's so-called gospel. Guilt for enjoying "unholy" pleasures. Guilt for marrying outside the church, then guilt for divorcing. Guilt for skipping church, guilt for attending the wrong church, guilt for questioning the church. And finally, when people muster the courage to leave the church, guilt for doing so.

When I first became a pastor, I did so with little theological reflection. The people in my church were kind, and I appreciated the Quaker testimonies of simplicity, peace, integrity, and equality. Being in community with people who valued those virtues seemed a fitting way to spend my life. That particular congregation didn't speak much about salvation, so I didn't think my job would be to get people into heaven. What I couldn't foresee was the cultural trend toward evangelical Christianity, which would cause a shift in my denomination's priorities. It would no longer be enough to emphasize the Quaker testimonies. Now my chief responsibility would be to get the meeting's children and youth saved through a personal relationship with Jesus Christ.

I wasn't quite sure how to do that, and to be honest I didn't have much enthusiasm for the task. I had grown up in a tradition that emphasized sin and the need for salvation, hadn't found it helpful, and had resolved to leave it behind. But I was young, unsure of my own theology, and began to experience feelings of guilt, wondering if I were jeopardizing the eternal well-being of the young people in my care by not getting them saved.

As I was wrestling with this matter, a church in our community extended an invitation for our town's teenagers to participate in a concert and worship service on a Sunday evening. I believed this event might be of some help to our youth, so I urged them to attend the event with me. In a word, the service was dreadful. The pastor summoned a teenage girl forward, then announced to hundreds of her peers that she'd had inappropriate sexual activity with her boyfriend. The girl burst into tears. I now believe she had confided in the pastor, only to suffer his betraying her confidence and using her for the opening illustration of his sermon. The pastor asked her for details in a manner that now strikes me as voyeuristic. I felt deeply sorry for the girl, was angry with the pastor, gathered the youth in my care, and left.

Others present at that event were also upset. Like me, they believed the pastor had betrayed a confidence, humiliated a young lady, and damaged the church's credibility. What no one questioned was the underlying theology behind the event, only the appropriateness of the minister's actions with one so young. I now believe what he did so blatantly is done a thousand times over in more subtle ways—the intentional use of shame to accomplish the church's objectives.

For some time, I wondered whether I should leave the church since I couldn't affirm what others told me were its central tenets. When I shared my misgivings with other Christians, it was often suggested I was spiritually deficient. I remember one conversation with a Christian acquaintance who admonished me for my hard-heartedness, saying the pastor had acted on God's behalf to bring the girl to repentance. There have always been Christians who dogmatically insist they are the true followers of Jesus, and those same persons often have a knack for making others feel spiritually deficient. This caused me to wonder if there were a place in the church for me. Fortunately, as I contemplated leaving, I encountered other Christians who shared my unease with what passed for normative Christianity. While we had a high regard for the teachings of Jesus, we rejected the shame-based culture of the church and its tendency of elevating God at the expense of humanity.

What do I mean when I say the church is a shame-based culture? Simply this, that perhaps since its earliest days, a significant segment of the church has used the weapons of manipulation, shame, embarrassment, and disgrace to accomplish its purposes. There are, of course, exceptions to this. But far too often these weapons have been brandished in order to gain followers, power, influence, and obedience. Interestingly, this tendency has transcended theological boundaries. I have seen conservative churches use shame to push its congregants toward specific doctrines. I have seen shame used in progressive churches to coerce persons into certain behaviors. Whether shame was used to compel someone to accept Jesus or recycle makes little difference to the one being shamed.

A friend of mine attended a church for a number of years. The congregation was growing and had decided to erect a new building. My friend was supportive of the project, but because of a job loss, was unable to meet his pledge. After falling behind, he received a letter from the church reminding him of his commitment, urging him to fulfill his pledge, lest he "grieve the Lord" by having his name added to the list of delinquent givers. He wasn't sure what that meant, but he lived in a small town and feared his financial hardships would be publicly revealed. Because payment was impossible, and the threat of exposure humiliating, he quit the church and has never joined another.

Another friend moved to a new town and began attending a progressive church. Though he was a pacifist, his family had a history of military service. One Sunday, a church member made a derogatory comment about persons in the military. My friend tactfully noted that his father and grandfather had served in the military and were kind, gracious people whom he deeply admired. Word quickly circulated that he was a warmonger, and he found himself on the outs.

I know both of these men well. I would be honored to have them join the meeting I pastor, but their revulsion toward the church is now so deep that they are no longer interested in organized religion of any sort. After a lifetime in the church, they have said what I've heard countless others say, in one form or another—"I am weary of the church's efforts to manipulate and shame me." Worse, this shaming is often undergirded by biblical citations, a not-so-subtle reminder that we've disappointed not only our fellow beings, but God.

At the beginning of this chapter, I mentioned a telephone conversation with a man in which I suggested that not all of the Bible was helpful or appropriate. What I did not point out to the caller was the wide range of worldviews and perspectives found in the Bible. Whenever I hear someone talk about the biblical view of marriage, the biblical view of child rearing, or the biblical view of God, I wonder which biblical view they're referencing. A good number of Bible verses recommend polygamy, an arrangement most people don't have in mind when they speak in hallowed tones about the biblical view of marriage. We tend to root around in Scripture until we find a verse that supports our preference, then crown our view the biblical one, even when other verses contradict it. This is why theological claims purporting to be biblical must be given a careful examination.

Nowhere is this scrutiny more necessary than in the church's statements about human nature. I grew up steeped in the doctrine of original sin, which asserts that because of Adam's and Eve's disobedience, all humans thereafter were born in a state of sin. Popularized by Augustine, this has been a core tenet of the church and is the chief reason churches baptize infants—to erase the stain of original sin. Because the church has had centuries to expand and refine this doctrine, it is more sophisticated than my portrayal of it, but my summation is accurate.[1]

This is one of the greatest ironies in today's church. The very Christians who take full advantage of scientific and technological progress still insist the earth is a mere five thousand years old, still believe Adam and Eve were its first inhabitants, still believe their story provides a true and credible account of human history, nature, and destiny. While otherwise enjoying and relying upon the scientific advancements of modernity, they utterly reject those same insights when trying to understand their origins and make sense of the human condition. In the process, they strain logic, defy common sense, and do great harm to the concept of God's justice. After all, any god who would condemn billions of people to hell because the first couple sampled a bite of fruit seems at the very least eccentric, and at worst despotic.

This is not to say the Bible can't be of help in our quest for self-understanding. When one is able to clear the hurdle of literalism, many of the stories, myths, and proverbs in the Bible are meaningful. This is especially true of another creation story found in the Bible. There were several different authors of Genesis, two of whom penned differing creation stories. Preceding the Adam and Eve story, in the first chapter of Genesis there is another, more uplifting, creation story. The church, consistent with its culture of shame, emphasizes the negative account of Adam and Eve. Because many of us are biblically illiterate, because we are told Scripture speaks in a unified voice about human nature and origins, and because our priests and pastors speak with such authority, we assume that the Adamic version of creation they favor, with its twin themes of sin and guilt, is the biblical one, just as we assume there is only one biblical perspective of marriage or child rearing or God.

But consider for a moment a competing creation story found near the end of the first chapter of Genesis. I invite you to pause and read it, beginning with the twenty-sixth verse.

Then God said, "Let us make humankind in our image, according to our likeness; and let them have dominion over the fish of the sea, and over the birds of the air, and over the cattle, and over all the wild animals of the earth. . . ." So God created humankind in his image, in the image of God he created them; male and female he created them. God blessed them, and God said to them, "Be fruitful and multiply, and fill the earth and subdue it. . . ." God saw everything that he had made, and indeed, it was very good.

In that narrative, men and women were made in the image of God, urged to procreate, entrusted with the stewardship of creation, blessed by God, and pronounced good. The difference between this story and the Adam and Eve one is so vast as to be startling. The first story has men and women created simultaneously, suggesting equality. The second story has Eve created from Adam, implying subservience. The first story urges men and women to procreate, implying a divine blessing of sexual intimacy. The Adam and Eve story has them cowering in the garden, ashamed of their nudity. The first story suggests the characteristics of our relationship with God are wonder, trust, blessing, and love. The Adam and Eve story features disobedience, failure, punishment, and censure. In the language of the priest and writer Matthew Fox, one story is about original sin, the other about original blessing.

What would it mean if the church affirmed our potential rather than condemn our brokenness?

Religions tell us who we are. The myths and stories they pass on are critical in our moral and spiritual development and must be carefully chosen. Unfortunately, we often accept these stories uncritically, accepting their perspectives on human and divine nature without question. I mentioned the differences in the Genesis creation myths, which is but one example of the power of story to influence our worldview. Had the church chosen to emphasize the created-in-God's-image narrative, taking care not to literalize the story as a historic account, but stressing its themes of creative love, stewardship, and acceptance, it would have radically altered the church's message.

Because our spiritual ancestors were less than discriminating in the myths and stories they passed on, we find ourselves burdened with unpalatable doctrines we nonetheless feel pressured as faithful Christians to affirm and pass on. We recite creeds we no longer believe, teach these stories to our children with little or no interpretation, pray as if these doctrines are true, sing hymns that reinforce them, and support priests and pastors who use them to bludgeon the less powerful. Bad beliefs persist because the "true believers" who spread them have made dissent unpleasant and difficult. They persist because the popes, priests, and pastors who promise to deliver us from the grip of sin, enjoy the institutional power these myths and doctrines confer. But, chiefly, these negative, pessimistic worldviews persist because we the people have been too fearful and too compliant, too willing to endure the spiritual abuse they engender.

The first step in our movement toward healthy religion begins when we say, "Enough!" Enough guilt. Enough rejection. Enough fear. Enough assuming the worst about humanity and the worst about God. Enough cherry-picking the Bible stories that reinforce negative stereotypes and promoting them as "God's Word" to us. Enough twisting of words, calling bad news good news.

I know a woman who said "Enough!" to her church. She had been raised in a fundamentalist household, married a man with a similar religious perspective, had a daughter with him, and dutifully took her to church each Sunday. One Sunday morning, her minister delivered a sermon in which he explained why God wanted women to be subservient to men. She looked at her four-year-old daughter, realized the kind of world this man's words were creating for her child, and that afternoon told her husband she would no longer attend that church. Her husband resisted her newfound courage, citing various scriptures to support his argument, then finally demanded they meet with the pastor for counseling. To this, she consented.

The next morning, they met in the pastor's office. Their minister began by praying *at* the woman, asking God to soften her heart and bring her rebellion to an end. In the past, she'd buckled under such intimidation, but this time her resolve was deep. She laughed, told the men she would not be an accomplice in their efforts to subjugate her daughter, then informed them she would be looking for a new church where all people were valued.

The pastor soberly informed her he would be praying for her soul. She told him, and I quote, "My soul is just fine, thank you. In fact, it's never been better."

Unfortunately, her search for a healthier church proved more difficult than she'd anticipated. The area in which she lived was rife with dogmatic religiosity. After visiting half a dozen churches, she found one in a nearby city, led by a creative, encouraging pastor secure enough in her identity to let her parishioners find their own.

But the woman's emancipation came with a price. Most of her friends were affiliated with her former church. Their responses were similar to their pastor's. They urged her to end her disobedience, prayed aloud *at* her, and finally demanded she obey her husband, who, like them, was perplexed by his wife's refusal to "get right with the Lord." With good humor, but firm resolve, she persisted in her new direction, ultimately losing many of her old friends, but also making new ones. As for her marriage, it is fragile. Her husband belittles her religious choices, believes she has fallen under the control of Satan, and uses every occasion to mock her spiritual growth. I suspect she might one day say, "Enough!" to that too.

In churches where humans are seen as sinful, flawed, and broken, deviation from the doctrines is met with stiff resistance. The woman who challenged her church's misogyny discovered this. Even now, she is amazed at the number of women who willingly subject themselves to such maltreatment. So thorough is their indoctrination, they cannot envision a spirituality that doesn't also require their suppression. Regrettably, this disparagement of human nature isn't limited to women. I can't count the times I have sung a beloved hymn of the church, confessing to general wretchedness (*Amazing Grace*), sat mutely while ministers prayed for God to forgive me for sins I hadn't committed, and left worship services and Bible studies feeling spiritually and emotionally bruised.

But when churches and Christians take seriously our human potential, they begin creating communities that affirm and encourage all people. They give careful thought to the hymns they sing, rewriting the lyrics to better reflect God's inclusive love. Their prayers embody God's concern for all people and the delight and gift of human life and potential. They take seriously the power of human intellect and reason. Those communities care less about keeping men and women in their supposed God-appointed places and care more about the divine life present in all. For them, the Bible isn't a rule book of immutable laws. Rather, it is the unfolding drama of Israel's relationship with God. They believe the Bible is helpful and instructive, but certainly not exhaustive or ultimately authoritative. They are well aware that God has been fully present in other places, in other people. To that end, they believe God's reign is best served when people, and all of creation, are treated respectfully and graciously, with the appropriate freedom to discern their own paths and reach their full potential.

Too often the Bible is used to degrade the human spirit, often in an effort to save someone's soul. But what is salvation, what does it mean to have our souls saved? A primary concern for Jesus was helping others become mature—spiritually, ethically, emotionally, and relationally. The church has typically understood salvation as being rescued from our sin and going to heaven when we die. But what if we believed salvation was our lifelong journey toward maturity, love, and wholeness? Were that the case, Jesus would not be the one who saves humanity by his sacrifice of blood, but the one who exemplifies this maturity, love, and wholeness, the one to whom Christians can look and say, "This life is what it means to be saved, this is what it looks like to be fully human, and we can be like him!"

No longer viewing ourselves as wretched sinners, deserving of damnation, we could see ourselves and others as God does—beloved, accepted, valued, cherished, of infinite worth and potential. Churches would exist to help us comprehend and appreciate that reality, equipping and encouraging us to live freely, fully, and faithfully. Such a process would begin by recognizing the destructive potential of negative mythology, paying careful attention to the stories we valued and shared. These churches would think carefully of the community ethos they created and spread. They would call to positions of power those persons whose sense of God and self were appropriate and healthy. Leaders would not be valued for their ability to further the institution, but for their capacity to create soul-nurturing communities. Shame, blame, and spiritual tyranny would be things of the past, remnants of a fear-based religion whose precepts we have outgrown.

It is long past time for the flowering of a life-giving Christianity. Indeed, our future as a race might well depend on our willingness and ability to abandon the Christianity that divides and degrades us so we can embrace a new way of thinking about God and ourselves, a spirituality that more accurately reflects the values and priorities of Jesus.

I often receive letters, e-mails, or phone calls from persons looking for a life-affirming community. Weary and frustrated by their experiences with life-diminishing churches, they seek a gathering of persons whose theology is broad enough, whose hearts are loving enough, to accept people whose life experiences have brought them to different places. I have visited many such communities over the years. They defy easy categorization. I've met traditional Baptists in the South who were amazingly gracious and affirming, and I have felt unwelcome in progressive congregations whose denominational polity is radically inclusive. Just when I've been ready to dismiss an entire denomination as closed off and close-minded, I have encountered a loving, spiritually inquisitive, soul-affirming local community.

Ironically, these congregations are often well-kept secrets. I leave them, moved by their simple kindness, but scratching my head, wondering why their pews aren't packed. I'm mystified by the number of people willing to attend churches whose view of humanity is so warped and distorted that the congregants leave the service spiritually and emotionally bruised, only to return the next week for another dose.

I was once talking with a friend about the growth of a church in our area whose leadership was controlling and negative, with a keen eye for human failings.

"I can't believe people are willing to go there every Sunday to hear how bad they are," I said.

My friend said, "There will always be people willing to be told the worst about themselves. And there will always be churches eager to tell them."

But I am an optimist. I believe the day will come when shame-based churches will sit empty, when people will tire of hearing how sinful they are and will seek out communities of hope and goodwill, where the twin lights of God's grace and human potential brightly shine.

Let's consider, by way of hopeful example, how the themes of grace and potential were central to the ministry of Jesus. I think of his encounter with Zacchaeus,[2] a strong-arm tax collector whose traitorous alliance with the occupying powers caused his fellow Jews to brand him as a despicable sellout. Passing through the town where Zacchaeus lived, Jesus spied him in a tree, where Zacchaeus had climbed for a better view. Stopping, Jesus urged him to climb down and open his home so they could share a meal. This scandalized those present, whose culture forbade table fellowship with known sinners. Zacchaeus, touched by Jesus's welcoming gesture, was spontaneously inspired to return all he had stolen and more.

The radical response of Zacchaeus underscores the contempt in which he was held by his neighbors. Accustomed to scorn and rejection, the gracious hospitality of Jesus spurred him to respond with grace, integrity, and dignity. Though nothing more is ever told of Zacchaeus, it is intriguing to speculate about the changed direction of his life. I see a man once so enslaved by greed that he cheated those closest to him, now liberated from selfishness, sharing with the poor, opening his home, pouring out his life. Because every previous effort to "save" him was so rooted in shame, the gracious invitation of Jesus shifted Zacchaeus's world, and he could do little else but respond in an equally dramatic manner, giving back four times what he had stolen.

Could Jesus's spirit of generosity be replicated in our churches? Could our churches become communities where belief in human transformation and potential come naturally and instinctively? While our churches would not be blind to human brokenness and failings, neither would we believe such failure to be the whole measure of one's life. In the gospel of Luke,[3] a parable is told about two men who went to the temple to pray. The first man, a religious leader, thanked God he was not like his fellow prayer, a known cheat. But the other man envisioned a larger life for himself and asked for mercy and a fresh start.

For too long, the church has prayed like the first man, seeing only sin in others and being blind to their promise. The church true to the spirit of Jesus is the church that can see beyond human sin, speak to our deep hunger for mercy and redemption, and give us a vision for all the glory and goodness we could be.

1. Because theologians inherit the theologies of the past, much of our work consists of making ancient doctrines more palatable rather than admitting our spiritual ancestors might have been mistaken. For years, I tried to make the doctrine of original sin sound reasonable. It can't be done.
2. Luke 19:1–10.
3. Luke 18:9–14.

If the Church Were Christian . . .

Reconciliation Would Be Valued over Judgment

One of my earliest memories of the church was the sacrament of confession, which was held on Saturday evenings at the small Roman Catholic church my family attended. I would stand in line with my brothers and sister, waiting my turn to tell the priest the sins I'd committed that week. Because I was so young, around seven years old, I didn't understand what constituted sin, so would confess the same misdeeds each week—fighting with my brothers and disobeying my parents. For those offenses, I would have to perform the same acts of contrition, repeating two brief, memorized prayers.

I went to confession nearly every week until I was in my midteens. For as long as I went, the priest and I never deviated from our pattern. I confessed the same sins, he assigned the same sanctions, and I left the church ostensibly free from the charge of sin. These many years later, I wonder if the priest ever tired of my weekly repetitions. He never urged me to think more deeply about the nature of sin, forgiveness, and reconciliation. To be fair, I had little tolerance for introspection, so even if he had urged me to be more reflective, I would have been ill-suited for the task.

Though I never thought of it then, my experience with confession seems now to have been largely vertical. The emphasis was on how I had grieved God, with no mention of how I might improve relations with my fellow humans. God was the offended party, the one from whom forgiveness must be sought. Fortunately, spats with my brothers grew rarer as we matured, and today we're close. Perhaps the priest realized this, chalked up our disputes to a sibling rivalry we would outgrow, and elected not to fix something that wasn't broken. Unfortunately, it made me think forgiveness and reconciliation were private matters between God and me—that as long as God was appeased, little else mattered.

The other consequence of my confessional experience was the emerging perception I had of God. I came to believe God's priorities were skewed, that in a world plagued by war, famine, and cruelty, God was most concerned that I had bickered with my little brother, and not just concerned, but angry, willing to send me to hell over this trifling matter. A friend's father was an alcoholic with a hair-trigger temper and prone to violent outbursts over the slightest offense. His wife and children walked on eggshells in his presence, going out of their way to appease him, lest he erupt. God seemed to me to be much like that man, thin-skinned, easily angered by trivial affairs, reacting to events far out of proportion to their importance.

The church of my youth, rather than counteracting this perception, allowed it to persist and even perpetuated it, communicating in varied ways that God was angry and impulsive, as likely to curse as to bless. This theological tendency wasn't limited to my church. Indeed, God's judgment was (and remains) a dominant theme in much of Christianity, whose preaching and teaching were designed to assuage God's wrath and secure God's favor. Of course, when the goal of religion is appeasement, fear escalates, judgment increases, reason and mercy fall by the way, and all manner of absurd "solutions" arise to placate God. In traditional Christian theology, the solution to God's theoretical wrath was to satisfy it with the gruesome, cruel death of Jesus, which somehow mollified God, allowing God to forgive and bless us. Consequently, another feature of my early religious training, in addition to the regular confession of my sins, was the reminder to continually praise and thank Jesus for interceding with God on my behalf.

In addition to its dreadful view of God, another unfortunate effect of appeasement theology was the power it gave those who claimed to represent God and asserted their authority to extend divine forgiveness, namely, the church and its leaders. In the Middle Ages, the church amassed vast riches, conferring forgiveness and salvation only after generous donations

Philip Gulley

had been made. This was known as the sale of indulgences. One of the more creative preachers of that era, Johann Tetzel, was fond of saying, "As soon as a coin in the coffer rings, the soul from purgatory springs." He created a list of sins, each one bearing a specific financial penalty. Were you to visit the Vatican and tour St. Peter's Basilica, you would be standing in a structure constructed from the sale of indulgences. Today the church is more subtle, but one gets the impression, when listening to certain preachers, that a donation of the right amount, slipped into the right hand, will secure God's favor.

I can't help but think our misunderstanding of divine mercy has distorted our understanding of human forgiveness. In my years as a pastor, I've met with many persons for spiritual direction. Time and again, the issues that bring them to my door have to do with forgiveness and reconciliation—husbands and wives estranged from each other, parents and children no longer speaking or sharing meals, families torn asunder by long-ago slights—the gall and bitterness still fresh, neighbors at odds, friendships riven by misunderstandings, and churches split by theological dissension.

I know a couple whose estranged daughter was dying of a terminal disease. I loved each of the persons involved and hoped for their reconciliation before the daughter's passing. The parents made several overtures but were turned away when they came to visit their dying daughter. (Several years before, the daughter and her sister had quarreled, the parents had refused to take sides, advising their grown children to work out their differences peaceably. The daughter felt betrayed and resolved never to speak to her parents again.)

I thought of bringing the daughter and parents together in hopes of a reconciliation. But the daughter's bitterness was so deep and sharp, I lacked the nerve to challenge her. In her final months, the daughter spoke often of her Christian faith and how it sustained her, while seemingly blind to one of that faith's bedrock principles—forgiveness.

Before she died, she left strict instructions that her parents and siblings were forbidden from attending her funeral. The mother and father, mystified and heartbroken by their daughter's intransigence and not wishing to anger her spouse, stayed home to mourn privately.

I have reflected on that experience many times since, trying to understand the depth of the daughter's anger and my own unwillingness to address it. I have seen similar situations play out in churches, when hostility between persons was so entrenched and powerful it poisoned the community. Lines were drawn, sides were chosen, every issue within the church affected by the enmity. The disagreements became so venomous, to touch them was to die. On one occasion, I found it easier to leave a church than deal with the toxic power of division.

Thankfully, I have also witnessed incredible acts of reconciliation. A fellow Quaker took issue with my theology and publicly demanded my expulsion from our denomination. He did so in a strident manner, which many people found distressing. To his credit, and I still marvel at the grace and strength this act required, he had a change of heart, visited my Quaker meeting, rose to his feet, and publicly apologized to me and my congregation. Several persons came forward to embrace him, and when he departed, he left with our profound respect and goodwill.

I have related this story when speaking with other Christians, and their reaction is universal. They are deeply moved and somewhat surprised, which makes me suspect reconciliation in the church is not as common as one would hope. Indeed, whenever I've spoken with people who've left the church, their disenchantment almost always was with the church's culture of judgment, citing examples of hostility their churches seemed unable or unwilling to heal.

When I became a pastor, I never imagined one of the more difficult aspects of the job would be the work of reconciliation. Like many pastors, I overestimated the power of eloquence, believing if I preached the right words or cited the appropriate scripture, hearts would soften and fractured relationships would mend. I have entertained visions of estranged factions standing in church, offering or asking forgiveness, and being reconciled, but that has seldom happened. Jesus had a similar hope, telling his followers that before they offered any gift to God, they should first offer the gift of reconciliation to others (see Matthew 5:23–24).

It is, I have learned, far easier to ask forgiveness of a god we can't see than from a person we can see. Perhaps this is why many religions are vertical in nature, focused on pleasing and placating God. That orientation has usually entailed sacrifice, the notion of giving God something—our time, our attention, our praise, our skill, our money—and, in extreme instances, our children, our virgins, an animal, our lives, or someone else's life. But early in his public ministry, Jesus articulated a different understanding of sacrifice—the surrender of pride, the surrender of ego, the surrender of the privilege of being right, the surrender of everything that keeps us estranged from others, so we can be reconciled.

True reconciliation is difficult, requiring vulnerability, honesty, and humility. These virtues should be commonplace in the church but are often lacking. Indeed, the twelve-step groups that meet in church basements take reconciliation more seriously than many in the church, speaking the language of grace more fluently than those who claim it as a first language. The participants' willingness to rigorously examine their lives, seek forgiveness, and make amends to those they've harmed is a practice the church would do well to emulate, yet one to which we seem strangely resistant.

The church of my youth made an effort, in its practice of weekly confession, to teach its people the language of reconciliation, but for many it became a rote and meaningless ritual, devoid of power and honesty. It seemed sufficient to go through the motions of reconciliation, to effect the posture of contrition. Again, it seemed to me to be a mostly vertical experience, emphasizing the appeasement of God's wrath over the restoration of broken human relationships. While this focus was unfortunate, it at least invited us to regularly consider the ways in which we had hurt and failed others. Curiously, few Protestant denominations have ever elevated to the level of sacrament the regular practice of confession and reconciliation, an odd circumstance in light of Jesus's emphasis on the matter.

Sometimes it seems as if there is an aversion to reconciliation in the church, as if the church were the last place anyone would go when restoration is needed. This is especially evident when people are experiencing marital difficulties. I can only recall a handful of instances when a couple came to me hoping to avert a divorce. In most instances, I have been informed of decisions to separate long after they were made, too late to be of practical assistance. For a time I worried my parishioners didn't find me approachable, but other pastors have told me they were often the last to know of estrangements, that people seemed to find the church of little value when healing was needed and were often reluctant to trust the church with their brokenness, fearing, perhaps with good reason, that judgment and recrimination would be the church's response.

Our reluctance to reveal our frailties to the church is understandable, given the climate we've created. Judgment has always seemed part and parcel of the Christian experience. Even Jesus, who spoke movingly about forgiveness and reconciliation, used the language of judgment, condemning priests, scribes, and Pharisees. Ironically, he chided those groups most often for their judgmental attitudes, and with words of censure and rebuke predicted their ultimate separation from

God. What is less clear is whether Jesus actually said those things, or whether those words were placed in his mouth, reflecting the growing discord between the Jewish people and the emerging Christian community. Whichever the case may be, Jesus or his earliest followers were well versed in the language of recrimination.

Like Jesus, the apostle Paul was capable of great tenderness. The thirteenth chapter of 1 Corinthians, even after two millennia, is still stirring and relevant. It is hard to believe that touching chapter was written by the same man who urged those who disagreed with his theology to castrate themselves (see Galatians 5:12). This reveals the dichotomy of the Christian Scriptures, whose pages justify both compassion and cruelty. Christians wishing to condemn and exclude can find justification in their Scriptures. When those same Scriptures are elevated as God's inerrant words, such condemnation appears virtuous and God-ordained. This is the state in which we find ourselves today—judgment and blame are believed by many to be God's will, the tools by which God's holy purposes are accomplished, and in that odd equation, coldness is treasured as much as compassion.

What would it mean if the church valued reconciliation over judgment?

Several years ago, an acquaintance phoned my home. Though she was not affiliated with the Quaker meeting I was serving, she was familiar with our beliefs and sympathetic to them.

She and her husband, unable to bridge their disagreement about whether to have children, had decided to divorce after ten years of marriage. I knew and liked both persons, was saddened by their impending divorce, and expressed my concern for them. But I also realized the difference between them was significant and unlikely to be resolved. In a perfect world, they would never have married individuals whose goals were incompatible with their own, but attraction, sexuality, and our need for partnership are powerful forces and not always receptive to reason. Fortunately, they were parting amiably, and were curious to know if I might be willing to conduct a ceremony that would dissolve their marriage while affirming their continued friendship.

I had never been asked such a thing, was initially uncomfortable with the idea, and though I kept my feelings to myself, I considered a ritual affirming divorce to be an inappropriate activity for the church. I asked her to give me some time to reflect on whether and how I might conduct such a ceremony, then urged her to phone me in a few days so we could discuss the matter more fully. Perhaps sensing my misgivings, she didn't phone again. She and her husband parted, their divorce proceeded along conventional lines, and neither of them raised the issue with me again. Their initial hope that they might remain friends was not realized, and while their divorce was not as contentious as some, neither did it proceed on the high note they had envisioned.

Though they had elected not to pursue a divorce ceremony, I continued to wrestle with the issue, reflecting especially on the sad consequences of adversarial divorce—emotionally traumatized children, embittered men and women, financial hardship, drug and alcohol abuse, sexual promiscuity, broken friendships, disruption in living arrangements, and other difficulties. Given those realities, I concluded that any effort the church could make to ease the pain of an inevitable divorce would be worthwhile.

I recall at the time speaking with a church elder about this topic, sharing my conclusion that it might be fitting for the church to create a ritual or ceremony that would publicly acknowledge divorce and minister to those affected by it.

"After all," I said, "the church was there when the marriage was begun. It seems appropriate we be present at its conclusion. We celebrate life, and we help people cope with death. Why can't we celebrate marriage and also help people cope with its end?"

Her response was swift and strong. "That's precisely what is wrong with the church today. It doesn't stand for anything. Anything goes. We've got no business celebrating sin."

We spoke a few moments longer, neither one of us ceding ground. I continued to suggest the church had a redemptive role to play in this increasingly common dilemma, while she kept insisting the church should stand squarely on the side of marriage. As a fan of marriage, I shared her enthusiasm for the institution, which I made clear to her. Though her behavior was polite, it was evident she would resist any ritual she felt condoned divorce. I was also acutely aware that she had never personally experienced divorce, that her marriage and the marriages of her parents and children were intact. It is often only after we've experienced the pain of an event that the need for healing and resolution becomes apparent.

I have known Christians whose vocabulary for judgment was rich and full, but their dialect for reconciliation and forgiveness, limited. They could easily summon the words for condemnation but fell mute when words of pardon were needed. Consequently, they tended toward a moral rigidity that made the work of reconciliation difficult, if not impossible. Eventually, they began to understand Christianity as a set of inviolate moral laws, many of which bore little resemblance to the values and priorities of Jesus but seemed to them to be the very fulcrum of the faith. The early church, while still in its infancy, in a culture beset with war, tyranny, and deep human suffering, seemed most concerned about the genital foreskin and whether its presence disqualified a man from church membership.

This affinity for moralism is not confined to the Christian faith. One universal trait of all religions is the tendency of their adherents to confuse spirituality with morality, constructing extensive lists of sins, which lead inevitably to cultures of recrimination and judgment. As surely as night follows day, when people are morally rigid, they define more and more things as sinful and become less likely to forgive and reconcile. Cultivating a spirit of understanding and com-passion in such settings is often an uphill slog.

If the church valued reconciliation over judgment, it would have to surrender its fondness for black-and-white, either-or thinking. Our tendency of reducing the most difficult mat-ters to the simplest and starkest of terms cripples our ability to understand and appreciate the moral complexity inherent in many issues. Worse, it predisposes us toward language of hos-tility when sympathy and understanding are most needed.

When I was in my early twenties and active in the peace movement, a young Quaker I knew joined the military. At the time, I believed Christianity was primarily about paci-fism, so I criticized his decision to enter the armed forces. I told him he couldn't be Christian and a member of the military at the same time. I cited precedent from our Quaker tradition, pointed out the moral incongruity of his decision, and predicted he would come to regret the path he'd chosen. Unfortunately, I was so strident that were he to have had mis-givings, he would have been loath to admit them. This is the problem with judgment—while it attempts to change behav-ior, its very nature often precludes a change of heart or mind, ultimately encouraging the very activity it seeks to curtail.

As a young minister, I had a high opinion of myself, which caused me to adapt a condemnatory attitude toward others. Just when I was on the verge of becoming insufferable, I was invited to pastor an urban Quaker meeting in Indianapolis. Though modest in size—there were twelve people present my first Sunday—they were compassionate and loving and had an easy, unaffected manner, which appealed to me. I hadn't been there long before sensing that the chief reason for the congregation's gracious spirit had to do with a couple who'd help found the congregation years before. Their names were Lyman and Harriet Combs. When I met them in 1990, they were retired and had devoted their remaining years to caring for others. Lyman volunteered each day at a homeless shelter, and Harriet made it her practice to be available to anyone in need. She babysat, transported people to appointments, tended the sick, visited the lonely, and did so with such transparent joy and good humor that to be in her presence was a redemptive experience.

Over the years, the meeting they had helped found took on their demeanor. A light, buoyant spirit infused the meeting's worship and activities. The meeting was incredibly generous, regularly emptying its bank account to help the less fortunate. Because of our close proximity to several resources for the homeless, we were often visited by mentally ill persons, all of whom were warmly welcomed and made to feel at home. In my nine years there, I would encounter persons who'd once attended the meeting. Their assessment was universal—"I attended that church when I was really down, and they helped me." When people would learn I pastored that church, they would tell of stumbling upon that Quaker meeting after a divorce, the death of a loved one, or some other painful experience and finding comfort, strength, and hope.

As gracious as the people were, I was often frustrated by their seeming indifference when it came to church growth. On one occasion, frustrated that the meeting wasn't growing as quickly as I'd hoped, I asked Harriet why that was.

"I guess it was never our goal to have a large church," she said.

Our denomination spent considerable resources trying to attract new attendees to our congregations, so I was taken aback by Harriet's response, which contradicted our denominational priority. I was also young and energetic and harbored a not-so-secret desire to pastor a growing Quaker meeting.

"Then why are we here?" I asked Harriet.

"To love," she said, smiling.

She didn't elaborate, and I didn't press her for a further explanation. But I contemplated her response, even as I continued to gauge our success by our Sunday attendance, assessing the numbers like an investor tracking the Dow Jones. In due time our membership grew, but I observed that our most joyful moments were those times when people extended healing to others. When numeric growth was our primary goal, we seemed to value only those persons who could contribute toward that aim—the financial donors, the families with children, the attractive, the gifted, the influential, and the capable. However, it took me a while to learn this, so while I was busily occupying myself with church growth, Harriet went cheerfully about the work of love—never excluding, never gauging the worth of people before caring for them, never judging another person, only working toward his or her wholeness and well-being.

Her aptitude for reconciliation—of restoring persons to fullness of life without condemnation—was so appealing that everyone aspired to be like her. She exemplified the saying attributed to anthropologist Margaret Mead, "Never doubt that a thoughtful, committed individual can change the world. Indeed, it's the only thing that ever has." The world Harriet changed was our church.

Time and again, I have seen the culture of a church transformed by the steady, gracious example of a single person. At key moments in a church's life, someone chose to act graciously, and that decision functioned like an electrical transformer, stepping up the current and flow of goodwill and compassion. Healthy, loving churches magnify a gesture of grace, transforming it into a mind-set and then a movement, expanding its power and presence. Unfortunately, decisions to judge and exclude can be equally contagious, sharing the same capacity for expansion.

Churches that value reconciliation over judgment and acceptance over condemnation get that way by choosing wisely at key moments, never losing sight of their purpose—to bring wholeness to broken lives, immersing each person and situation in God's grace. Jesus did this time and again, transforming people and situations by his gracious presence. While many in the church are acquainted with the stories of healing found in the New Testament, not many of us realize the social estrangement experienced by the sick and diseased in Jesus's day. Because illness and disease were indications of God's disfavor, the sick were often forced from home, made to wander from place to place at the mercy of others. To be healed was not only to be restored to health, but to be restored to family and friends, which was often the greater need.

One of the more poignant healing stories can be found in the seventeenth chapter of Luke's gospel. Ten lepers "who stood at a distance" (note the tone and manner of exclusion: lepers were required by law to stand at a distance from everyone) called out for Jesus to have mercy on them. Rather than judging them or speculating about what secret sin might have caused God's disfavor, Jesus healed them. In that one act, he restored not only their diseased bodies but their broken families as well. Indeed, so eager were the lepers to be reunited with their families that only one of the ten took time to return to Jesus and express thanks. In a delicious twist, the one who thanked Jesus was a foreigner, a Samaritan, the person others thought least likely to do the right thing. This was another element common in the ministry of Jesus—the people most estranged and excluded were often the very ones to model faithfulness, gratitude, and grace.

If the church were Christian, it would take seriously the reconciling example of Jesus. We know this. No one ever began attending a church intending to judge and condemn a fellow being, but the temptation is a strong one, and ungracious traits can be as infectious as good ones. Redemptive churches exercise the gifts of diagnosis, treatment, and healing. Judgmental churches dwell on the diagnosis, eager to point out a malady but incapable of effecting a cure. I have been blessed in my life to encounter both types of churches. They each taught by example, one by showing me what I didn't want to be, and the other by showing what I could be. The first taught me to judge, which I learned to do well. The second taught me to redeem, which I found more difficult, but infinitely more satisfying.

If the Church Were Christian . . .

Gracious Behavior Would Be More Important Than Right Belief

In the first chapter, I mentioned how the church's preoccupation with right belief or orthodoxy often comes at the expense of grace. I want to explore that topic more fully for two reasons. First, many of the disagreements Jesus experienced with the religiously rigid had to do with their fixation on orthodoxy, to the extent it made them blind to human suffering. Jesus knew ungracious behavior often had its roots in a misguided quest for theological purity. He also knew people of faith sometimes viewed this mistreatment as God-ordained, causing them to justify hardship as the consequence of sin. The second reason I wish to examine this subject more closely is because the tendency to value orthodoxy over grace is still with us, still misshaping our lives and the lives of others, still leaving us insensitive to human need, and still causing many kind and thoughtful people to reject the church as a compassionate community to which they might belong.

Several years ago I entered a local restaurant to eat lunch. It was noontime, and the restaurant was full, but as I turned to leave, an older gentleman seated by himself invited me to join him. I knew him mostly by reputation, that he was quite intelligent and tended to be outspoken but was also capable of great kindness. I also knew he had identified himself as an agnostic, if not an atheist. So when he invited me, a pastor, to join him for lunch, I was a bit surprised but also grateful for the opportunity to know him better.

Because I was his guest, I wanted to steer the conversation toward topics that might interest him, so I asked him about his new home, recently built outside of town in a wooded setting.

"It's just a house," he said, swatting away the topic as one would a pesky fly. "What I want to know is why you became a pastor."

I gave him my stock reply—that I was in it for the money.

He laughed, then said, "No, really. I really want to know."

I told him I found the study of theology interesting, that I valued the sense of community a church provided, and that helping others navigate life was meaningful to me.

"I don't believe in God," he said. "Would I be welcome in your church?"

"Certainly," I told him.

"Would I eventually have to believe in God in order to stay there?"

I thought for a moment before answering him. "If some people discovered you didn't believe in God, they might try to convert you. If they couldn't, they might grow upset with you. But as a pastor, I don't think belief can be compelled. I only care about your beliefs insofar as they affect your behavior. Given that, I would prefer a congregation of kind atheists over a congregation of hateful Christians. But," I added with a smile, "if you became a kind Christian, I would not be disappointed."

Our lunch arrived and we ate, moving easily from one topic to another. He was an engaging conversationalist, and I was enjoying our time together. After our meal was finished and the waitress had cleared our dishes away, I thanked him for inviting me to join him and expressed the hope we might enjoy another meal in the near future. We paid our bills, walked out of the restaurant together, and paused to say good-bye.

"You know," he said. "I love the theory of the church. It's the practice of it that leaves me cold."

His statement intrigued me, so I asked him to be more specific.

"I can't take the hypocrisy," he said.

I said hypocrisy in the church also bothered me and readily admitted that my own conduct was often inconsistent with my professed beliefs, but that I hoped my being in a Christian community might make me a more integrated person.

"Good luck," he said, smiling. "But I think I'll just stay a humanist."

I have recalled our conversation several times, not because of its uniqueness, but because of its common refrain, one I've heard again and again over the years—the disconnect between the conduct of the church and its stated beliefs.

I can't help but wonder if the chief cause of this disconnect, other than human frailty, is the church's obsession with orthodoxy over practice. Perhaps when the church was young, it was a matter of some importance to formulate a coherent, shared theology around which the church could unite. But as the church has grown and evolved, it seems to me that our slavish devotion to orthodoxy has not served us well. We have been hidebound when flexibility would have been more fruitful, judgmental when compassion was needed.

When I was a young man, I was eager to discern my life's goals and priorities, believing this clarity of purpose would provide the necessary framework for my life. Initially, I was very dogmatic, believing any deviation from my principles and values would be catastrophic. Like many true believers, I thought the only things holding the universe together were my moral and spiritual diligence. This understanding caused me to reject out of hand any theology or philosophy different from my own, even to the point of rudeness and hostility.

Eventually, I discerned other moral and spiritual codes were as beneficial as my own; indeed some of them even seemed to be superior. This caused me to be more sympathetic to the opinions and experiences of others. I realized no one person or religion had the lock on truth, that the lines of ultimate reality were not as sharply drawn as I had imagined them to be. I came to this conclusion after observing that those persons whose worldviews were most rigid were often the most unhappy. Ironically, the firmness of faith they thought would bring them joy had a stifling effect, crippling their ability to respond creatively when their life circumstances changed. Angry that the world seemed indifferent to their priorities, their inflexibility led to bitterness, their intransigence to resentment.

Conversely, it seemed that those persons whose moral compass tended toward general themes instead of hard-and-fast rules were the most emotionally adaptable, joyful, and healthy. Faced with a challenge or problem, they would ask, "What does love (or integrity or faithfulness or compassion) require of me in this situation?" then craft a fitting, creative response. While they were every bit as "moral" or "spiritual" as their more rigid counterparts, they also realized the world paid little heed to their moral codes, requiring some flexibility on their part to meet and overcome the rising challenges of life.

I remember two families, both of whom were active in a congregation with me. One family was especially dogmatic, while the other family appeared to be more flexible. Within several years of each other, both families had teenage daughters who became pregnant out of wedlock. The first family reacted with anger, demanding the daughter marry the boy who'd impregnated her. They took their daughter's pregnancy personally, accusing her of tarnishing the family's reputation. Within a few years, the daughter divorced, and to this day remains emotionally distant from her parents. The second family, though initially shaken by their daughter's pregnancy, rallied around her, urged her to continue her education, and treated the father with respect and dignity; when the child was born, they joyfully welcomed the infant into their family.

Because the first family valued compliance and obedience above all else, they seemed unable to respond graciously and creatively when their daughter violated their religious norms, while the second family, because they treasured graciousness over moral codes, were well suited to respond lovingly when their daughter most needed them.

I have seen similar scenarios play out, often around issues of sexual behavior, religious belief, and theological conformity. I've often wondered how families like the first one become the way they are, especially as it relates to our spirituality. Perhaps when we first experience God's presence in our lives, the experience is so powerful we assume others' understanding of God must mirror our own. The emphasis shifts from the joy of experiencing God to the codified method by which others must experience the Divine. That tendency to define, and consequently limit, God's revelation is understandable and almost universal. Though fundamentalism has often been portrayed as a conservative phenomenon, it spans the theological spectrum. It happens wherever and whenever people insist that their way to the Divine is the superior path. Perhaps this spiritual rigidity is a necessary step in our moral and religious evolution, a phase through which we must journey on our way to a richer, more meaningful spirituality. What is troubling are the many people who seem quite committed to that rigid religion, even as it cripples their lives and relationships.

If rigid orthodoxy is a common road down which individuals travel, perhaps it is also a common pattern for institutions. What is orthodoxy, if not the church's effort to describe and define the reality of God, the church's insistence that all must experience God as it has? Though the formulation of creeds might have been a necessary step in the church's journey, it happened relatively early in the church's life, hindering the church's ability to evolve spiritually. It was akin to telling someone he had to arrive at the truth by the age of ten. In its rush to codify the faith, the church provided answers long before we knew what questions to ask. When we dared to ask questions, we were directed to the creeds and commanded not to stray from their boundaries.

The church's rush to form an orthodox theology had several unfortunate consequences: It discouraged honest seeking, branding as heretical any conclusions that contradicted the church's settled assumptions. And by suppressing theological exploration, it kept people spiritually underdeveloped, dependent on the church to supply meaning and define reality. While the creeds provide a theological snapshot of the third- and fourth-century mind-set, they may no longer offer a credible way forward for those interested in a faith that engages the heart and mind. For many people, common sense, reason, and intellectual advances have made these ancient assertions unpalatable.

I am certainly not the first to point out the pitfalls of a set-in-stone orthodoxy. In the Quaker tradition from which I hail, the concept of continuing revelation arose in order to widen the parameters of spiritual exploration. Believing God was not confined to the pages of Scripture nor bound by the formulations of the church, early Friends held that God could speak fresh words and provide new insights as our capacity to learn and grow evolved. But the appeal of orthodoxy is strong, and even in a tradition that has rejected creedalism and rigid orthodoxy, certainty has its advocates.

I once taught a class on Quakerism, discussing with the participants the principle of continuing revelation. "I'm all for that," a man said, "so long as it doesn't contradict the Bible."

I pointed out that the Bible was theologically inconsistent, written by many different authors with many different worldviews, and that having to conform our insights and beliefs to every verse would be impossible.

"Nevertheless," he said, "if God has anything new to say to us, we'll find it in the Bible."

"Then it wouldn't be new, would it?" I asked.

The man thought for a moment. "I guess not," he said.

"So God's words to us are confined to the Bible?"

"Yes, that's right."

"That would mean there's no need for continuing revelation," I said.

"I don't see the need for it," he said, changing his mind in the span of thirty seconds.

This is the curious fix in which the church finds itself today. Even as we are uncomfortable with the confining nature of orthodoxy, we are loathe to live or think outside of it. We desire a fresh, relevant experience of God but fear any insight beyond our creeds and Scriptures, believing it will be unfaithful or even sinful. But how can our desire to grow and evolve be wrong? How can our wish to improve upon past teachings be displeasing or threatening to God? In every other endeavor, we welcome the advancements of science, careful thought, and progress. But in theology we not only fear such advancements, we condemn them.

While in college and seminary, I studied the views of ancient thinkers but was seldom encouraged to build upon them. The emphasis was placed squarely on memorizing the ideas of persons long dead. While history is a vital element in any field, in the discipline of theology it played (and plays) an excessive role. It was possible to be a star student by regurgitating past orthodoxies, without bothering to make them relevant or credible to the modern world. Though a few professors encouraged me to move beyond the boundaries, originality was generally frowned upon. I believed then, and still do, that any undertaking that discourages innovation and progress is bound to fail. It will fail precisely because it will be unable to attract the caliber of persons it needs to sustain and enrich its shared life.

This aversion to modernity seems to be unique to theology. If our doctor rejected out of hand the medical advances of the past three hundred years, we would quickly find a new doctor. If a United States president wished to place America under the rule of the British monarchy, he or she would be impeached. If a corporation employed children in barbaric conditions, ignored the rules of safety, and poisoned our land and waterways, it would be penalized. But take an ancient doctrine, insist it originated with God, devise a ritual that reinforces it, wrap it in a prayer, reward those who perpetuate it, and condemn to hell those who don't, and what you have is a significant portion of today's church.

In addition to making the church and those in it spiritually backward, this stubborn commitment to past ideologies can encumber our capacity to be gracious. I am reminded of the several instances when Jesus was condemned for violating a Sabbath law in order to heal the lame or blind. When faced with an opportunity to extend grace to a hurting person, the religionists of Jesus's day chose law over compassion. Not just once, but with chilling regularity. What is it about religion that makes otherwise kind people forsake the obvious good to uphold doctrines that have long lost their meaning?

What would it mean if the church valued gracious behavior over right belief?

While in my midtwenties, I was visiting a church in another denomination. Quaker worship tends to be simple, but this church belonged to a tradition whose pattern of worship was much more complex. I had studied this denomination enough to appreciate the rituals, and the experience was a positive one. I was especially impressed with the pastor, who engaged the congregation in a thoughtful and joyful manner. After worship I lingered to express my appreciation for his words and spirit.

In front of me, waiting to speak to the pastor, was a woman who was visibly agitated, as if she'd just experienced a loss, which, in fact, is what had happened. She explained to the pastor that her father had died a few days earlier, he hadn't belonged to a church, and she was worried about his destiny.

"He would have joined the church if he'd known he was going to die," she said.

As I listened to her speak with the pastor, I sensed she was mentally troubled. The minister perceived this also and reached out to take her hand and comfort her. The woman began to cry, lamenting the loss of her father.

"I never met your father," the pastor said, "but it sounds like he was a good man."

The woman nodded her head in agreement.

"In very special circumstances, the church grants membership to persons after they've passed away," the pastor said. "Let's do that for your father." He began to pray for the woman, expressing appreciation for her father's life, and then announced to the woman that her father was now a member of the body of Christ and a recipient of God's care and concern. The woman's demeanor changed dramatically. The fear went out of her eyes, she hugged the minister, and left the church grateful and unburdened.

I was left standing alone with the pastor. I expressed appreciation for the worship service, then asked, with a bit of a smile, "Does the church really give membership to dead people?"

"Not that I know of," he said. "But perhaps every now and then it's the right thing to do, don't you think?"

That event stands out in my memory as a Christ-filled moment. A woman in deep anxiety for a loved one received assurance of God's love for her father. Some pastors would have been all too eager to explain why membership wasn't possible in those circumstances. But this minister sensed the sacramental meaning of membership—the outward symbol of the inward reality of belonging and acceptance—and conferred it in order to bless and encourage another. I am grateful to have witnessed such largeness of spirit early in my pastoral career. It reminded me then, and still does, of the primacy of grace in the Christian story.

My experiences in ministry have been largely positive. I have encountered some of the brightest, kindest people anyone could hope to meet. Curiously, the relatively few bumps I've encountered have invariably involved persons whose unbending commitment to rules and doctrine has blinded them to grace and mercy. At critical points, they preferred Sabbath law over liberation and healing. Not only did they favor law over love, they insisted others make the same choice, thwarting the work of grace in the church. When I witnessed the pastor confer membership on a deceased man, I was acutely aware that if a lover of law had been present, the pastor would likely have had to answer for his kindness to the woman.

As I read the Gospels, I do not sense Jesus was an anarchist, wanting to overthrow the established order. He did appear to be a frequent and enthusiastic participant in the life of the temple and synagogue, which leads me to believe he found great meaning in the religious life of his day. I do think his charisma, coupled with his regular appeals for mercy above law, caused those in power to suspect him of anarchy. But it seems obvious he didn't want to jettison the entire Jewish tradition. He likely understood the importance of rules and process but was able to place them in their proper context, not giving them such weight that he was unable to act charitably when circumstances required it.

An example of Jesus's balance of grace and law is found in the gospel of John, in the fifth chapter. Jesus is heading toward Jerusalem to participate in a Jewish feast (again, note his participation in the religious tradition). While in Jerusalem he encountered a man—blind, lame, and paralyzed—

who'd waited many years to be healed beside the pool of Bethzatha, a site where others had been cured. Jesus spoke to the man, asking him if he wanted to be healed. The man replied affirmatively. Jesus commanded him to pick up his bedroll and walk. The man did so and was immediately healed. This took place on the Sabbath, the day of rest when faithful Jews were forbidden to work. But Jesus, caught between grace and religious law, chose mercy over right belief. He did this not once, but regularly, not because he scorned the tradition, but because he was able to assign matters their proper weight.

The balance between law and grace might well be the start of religious wisdom, discerning when rules must be followed, and when they must be laid aside so a greater good can be accomplished. Jesus did this so deftly, so skillfully, it boggles the mind to think there were those who objected. Who can't read the parable of the Good Samaritan and not appreciate Jesus's ability to teach deep truths consistent with the Jewish tradition while also causing his hearers to think of faithfulness in new ways. But if grace and goodness are possibilities for us, so is a preoccupation with edicts and commands. Our lives are a playing field where the two impulses contend, often on an unconscious level, so that even as grace and law battle within us, we are not aware of their struggle or even their effect.

The Christian life is an invitation to awareness, to be mindful of our rightdoings and wrongdoings, our deeper impulses and motives. Valuing gracious behavior over right belief begins with awareness, our willingness to temporarily suspend a good thing (doctrine) so we can be faithful to a better thing (grace). Grace, since it is not instinctive, begins with mindfulness and our deliberate intention to act with loving kindness when we could have justifiably done otherwise.

I know a congregation who spent two years discerning whether they would conduct same-gender marriages. They were acutely aware that some persons would leave if they conducted gay marriages, and others would leave if they didn't. Nevertheless, they believed the issue was worth the difficulty, so they proceeded thoughtfully and carefully, studying the Scriptures, educating themselves about human sexuality, talking with gays and lesbians, listening carefully to one another, and praying.

Through this period, I met occasionally with the pastor, who filled me in on their progress. I marveled at her ability to remain nonanxious about a process that would have given me ulcers. Our conversations were lively and fun, and I looked forward to our discussions to learn of the congregation's progress. By the close of their discernment, the congregation had decided to affirm same-gender marriage. Interestingly, the experience was imbued with such grace that the handful of persons who disagreed with the conclusion remained committed to the church.

Because the process unfolded slowly, I had ample time to reflect on their situation from the sidelines. Specifically, I thought how the pace and tenor of their corporate life had facilitated their graciousness. So often, decisions made in haste don't allow proper time for our better angels to lend their voices. Bias and ignorance are always the first to raise their hands. Our first reactions are often strident, unthoughtful, and even uncaring, springing from our prejudices and prejudgments, untempered by consideration and compassion. Time tends to make us gracious. It gives us the opportunity to view a given situation from other angles and perspectives.

Time can be both a curse and a blessing. While the church can be swiftly impulsive in its intolerance, it has often taken long years to act graciously. Indeed, the church's reluctance to lead the way toward a broader loving kindness has often impeded our society's moral advancement. In some instances, the church has even furthered evil—defending slavery as God's will, condemning women to second-rate citizenship, labeling homosexuals as abominations, defining AIDS as a punishment from God, promoting war as an expression of God's will, justifying ill-gotten wealth as a blessing from the Lord, and suggesting poverty was a sign of divine rejection. Too many times, the church has been the caboose on the train of moral progress, at times a drag on grace and compassion.

Similarly, certain attitudes foster grace, while other attitudes diminish it. Dead seriousness and religious rigidity often go hand in hand. But when we can find the humor in a situation, even though the circumstances are very important, we give ourselves the necessary freedom to act more graciously than we otherwise might. Decisions aren't viewed as strict life-and-death matters but as steps along the way, which can be revisited if contrary evidence emerges.

Fear and seriousness are almost always the enemies of grace. Fear seizes control and demands compliance. Grace shares power and trusts others to make their own moral decisions. Fear is somber, stern, and uninspiring; grace is cheerful, joyful, and creative. Fear provides no room for error and is always in a hurry to have its way. Grace is expansive and gives us the time and space to learn and grow.

In his book *A New Earth*, spiritual teacher Eckhart Tolle writes, "Life isn't as serious as my mind makes it out to be."[1] When I first read those words, I felt an exhilarating sense of freedom and a keen awareness that life was to be appreciated and enjoyed. In sharp contrast, the church, which has always taken itself too seriously, has made us feel like our lives are in the balance, that we teeter on a precipice, our eternal well-being hanging on one decision, which must be made now, this moment, without delay. (The church will finally be faithful to Jesus when we feel the same urgency when faced with issues of justice and need.) The fears that escalate such gravity and gloom permeate the church, inhibiting our ability to live graciously and spontaneously.

Before my first theological book was published,[2] word of its universalist themes became known, and I found my pastoral credentials under threat of revocation. (This seems to happen with startling regularity. I write a book or give an

and a self-appointed guardian of the faith will take
my perspective and undertake efforts to punish
me.) Without exception, those clamoring the loudest for my
censure have been dead-serious, anxious to sever relationship
as quickly as possible, unwilling to view God or ultimate reality from any perspective but their own, and deeply fearful
the church would collapse were I to remain a part of it.

The antidote to this lethal mind-set is to remember that
when Jesus was asked to boil down the law to its essential
element, he didn't hesitate. Love. Love your neighbor. Love
the Lord. Love yourself. Jesus never, not once, went to the
mat for doctrine. Yet every split and schism in the church
happened because of our stubborn insistence that others must
profess the "right" beliefs. We have expended huge amounts
of resources and goodwill, defending the very aspect of religious life Jesus valued least. This is the great irony of Christ's
church—a significant number of its members care more
about believing certain things *about* Jesus, than following his
example of love and service. If the church were Christian,
mirroring the compassion of Jesus would be more important
than echoing the orthodoxy that has built up around him.

1. Eckhart Tolle, *A New Earth* (New York: Dutton, 2005), 33.
2. *If Grace Is True*, cowritten with James Mulholland and published by Harper-
   One in 2003.

5

If the Church Were Christian . . .

Inviting Questions Would Be Valued
More Than Supplying Answers

While in my midthirties, I was invited to speak at a church and had arrived early so I could attend their adult-education class. A famous person had died the day before, and when I entered the room, the class was discussing his career and death.

"Do you know if he was a Christian?" one of the ladies present asked.

No one seemed to be aware of the celebrity's religious orientation.

One of the men winced. "I sure hope he said the magic prayer," the man said with all sincerity.

I was confused by his remark and asked the man, "What's the magic prayer?"

"The one where he asked Jesus into his heart," the man said.

I was a guest and thought it impolite to question my host's comment, so I didn't say anything. But I believed it revealed an almost childish point of view. I later learned the man was a physician and had obviously pursued higher education but was effectively "stuck" in a theological position that hadn't changed since his early years.

Since that time, I have met many Christians like him—people who are otherwise curious and inquisitive, eager to expand their understanding of a particular topic, but apathetic when it comes to spiritual exploration. They found the "truth" early in life, accepted it without question, and resolved not to pursue it further. For them, the spiritual life consisted of the regurgitation of stock doctrines and pat answers. Their lethargy was enabled by clergy who discouraged any spiritual exploration that might result in a challenge to the spiritual status quo. But it persisted because many in the pews preferred the comfort of certainty over the growing pains that invariably accompany spiritual transformation.

Several years later I was invited back to that same church and, during the question-and-answer period, was asked whether I believed in the virgin birth of Jesus. It was near Christmas, perhaps an unwise time to challenge natal doctrines, but I answered honestly—that the doctrine of the virgin birth could not be supported biblically, that it arose in an unenlightened era when women and sex were understood to be inherently sinful, it made no scientific sense, and it added nothing to the stature of Jesus. I noted the doctrine of the virgin birth was as much a theological issue as it was a biological issue and persisted because it seemed to affirm the uniqueness of Jesus, but there were more credible ways to honor Jesus that didn't require the suspension of common sense. I concluded by saying that its perpetuation probably kept more people from embracing the Christian faith than it had ever attracted. I said all these things gently, knowing many present were hearing these things for the first time and might be troubled by my words.

Later that day my telephone rang. It was a woman from that church, asking to speak with me. We made arrangements to meet at my home the following day. When she arrived, she was visibly agitated and told me she hadn't slept the night before for thinking about my response.

"Now I don't know what to believe," she said. "If I can't believe the virgin birth, I can't believe anything."

I pointed out that while I didn't believe in the virgin birth, she was not required to agree, that many people in the church still believed it, and she was free to affirm it if she wished.

She asked me why I had questioned it in the first place, saying ministers should not cast doubt on the church's teachings.

I obviously disagreed. "The purpose of a spiritual teacher isn't to be a propagandist," I told her. "It's my responsibility to discern the truth. Sometimes, I agree with the church's historic conclusions; sometimes I don't. When I do agree, I will say so. When I don't, I will say so, and say why. But my goal will always be the discernment of truth." Again, I spoke kindly, in a noncombative but clear manner. I sensed her anxiety was diminishing and she was finding our conversation intriguing.

Then I returned to her original statement. "You said if you didn't believe the virgin birth, you can't believe anything. But I know many people who don't believe in that doctrine who have rich spiritual lives, who have a profound respect for Jesus, and follow his teachings with real devotion. In fact, I would like to consider myself one of them."

She began to tell me her spiritual biography. It was clear that disagreement with the church's doctrines was an option she had never thought possible. She'd been raised in a dogmatic church that discouraged any kind of theological inquiry, especially if that inquiry might lead one to an alternative conclusion. As an adult, she had chosen a similar church, led by an intellectually lazy pastor who repeated the same bromides Sunday after Sunday, effectively dulling the congregation's capacity to think, reflect, and grow.

As she was telling me her story, an image came to mind, which I shared with her as she was leaving. It was the image of a rose that had never been told it could blossom. The potential was there, the flower had budded, but always stopped just short of blooming. "I wonder why I thought of that image as you were speaking?" I asked.

I think I knew why that image came to mind, but I wanted her to wrestle with its possible meaning.

I didn't hear from her for several months, then saw her in a store. She was no longer attending that church. "In fact," she told me, "I'm not going to church anywhere."

"That, too, can be a necessary step in your spiritual journey," I said. "Use this time to explore, to think, to ask questions. You might even try a different denomination or even another faith."

She laughed. "One step at a time," she said. "I'm still having to get used to not being in church."

Eventually, she discovered a church whose leadership encouraged spiritual exploration, and she blossomed. When last I saw her, a new joy infused her life. "It's funny," she said. "My friends in my old church have told me I've left Jesus. But it feels like I've finally found him."

Unfortunately, this kind of spiritual maturation is not common. The church does an excellent job of rewarding the status quo and discouraging spiritual inquiry. In more extreme instances it shuns or disfellowships those who question or reject orthodoxy; in milder cases it makes disagreement so uncomfortable that would-be dissenters quickly learn to toe the party line. Ironically, many have found it necessary to leave the church in order to pursue serious spiritual illumination. How odd that the one institution that should prize the search for truth and enlightenment has decided that such a goal is not worthy of its best efforts and, indeed, is even threatening to its purposes.

But life is no respecter of ideology. The circumstances of life—suffering, struggle, illness, and death—have a way of revealing the absurdity of our tightly held religious claims. I know a man whose wife passed away after a year-long battle with cancer. They had attended a church for several years where they had been assured of God's ability to heal illness, and consequently they had spent many hours in prayer since the wife's diagnosis, asking God to cure her.

I saw the man at a store several weeks after his wife's funeral. He was bitter and angry.

"The funeral calling was terrible. All those people from church came through the line, telling me this was God's will, that God needed an angel, that God needed her more than I did, that she was better off. It was a load of crap. I'm done with church."

I placed my hand on his shoulder, told him how sorry I was about his wife's death, admitted I had said equally insensitive things to grieving people, then made plans to share a meal with him in a few weeks. When that day came, his anger had faded a bit, permitting us to talk about his loss in a more open manner.

I asked him why he'd been so angry at his fellow churchgoers. I was careful not to say it in an accusatory way. I was genuinely curious and wanted to learn.

He thought for a moment, then said, "I guess I'm mostly angry at myself. I used to say those same things. I'm angry that I never gave these things much thought and mad the church never asked me to. They gave me easy answers, which I accepted without thinking. Now that I need to make sense

of God and suffering, I don't know where to start. I guess I'm
mad because the church didn't teach me any better, and I'm
upset with myself for not insisting it should."

As soon as he said that, I remembered the many times
people in my church had approached me with profound
questions and I had offered shallow answers, evaded their
questions altogether, made light of them, or changed the
subject. I have seldom said, "I don't know the answer to your
question, but I'm willing to reflect on it with you." There is,
even after a quarter century of ministry, a deep need in me to
appear authoritative on spiritual matters. The words "I don't
know" don't come easily.

My discomfort with questions is not uncommon in the
church. For too long, the church has held itself up as the
expert on spiritual matters, quick to supply answers but not
altogether comfortable with questions or doubts. I remember
once hearing a minister comment, when asked about the existence of God, that it was a sin to question such matters.

When the British scientist and atheist Richard Dawkins
wrote *The God Delusion*, I recommended to a group of fellow
pastors that they read it. I pointed out that the book was on
the *New York Times* bestseller list and was likely being read
by persons in our congregations, so it might behoove us to
acquaint ourselves with it. One pastor read the book and
later thanked me, saying he'd found it helpful. Most of them
appeared uncomfortable with the idea of reading anything
written by an atheist. Two of the ministers wrote me e-mails

saying I was not qualified to serve as a pastor, and another minister speculated I had become possessed by demons. Those three pastors often voiced their confidence in God, attributing all number of things to God, affirming over and over their unshakeable faith in God, insisting others should believe as they did. Yet when invited to read one book that questioned their assumptions, these champions of faith reacted with what can only be described as fear.

This fear is pervasive in the church—fear the church's foundations are so rickety one well-placed question might bring down the house, fear someone might ask a question we can't answer, fear a sincere question might cause us to doubt what we've been taught. I have known these fears myself. The Quaker meeting I pastor has an adult-education class that addresses one theological or ethical question each Sunday. One week a man asked, "Is the church necessary?" I immediately felt anxious, tried to steer the conversation toward an affirmative conclusion, deeply fearful the group might decide the church wasn't needed and, by extension, that I wasn't needed. My motives were apparently so transparent that one man said aloud, "Sounds like our pastor is trying to protect his job." The others laughed. I started to object but realized he was right and laughed with them.

The unease I felt was real and common. Most of us do become anxious when asked whether our life's work has been worthwhile or necessary. Many times, our anxiety is manifested in anger and defensiveness. We resent people questioning our choices or conclusions and sometimes even attempt to punish them. Intellectually, we know such challenges might be helpful, nudging us toward a more reasoned, helpful faith. Emotionally, we feel threatened and become reactive, acting rashly. If we can remain nonanxious and still our fears long enough to entertain the question, we might discover the question was a gift to us, revealing a weakness that long hindered our growth and well-being. When the man asked whether the church was necessary, I was eventually forced to consider the merit of his question. I concluded that many aspects of the church weren't necessary. That dawning realization was one of the primary motives for this book. If I continue to keep that question before me, it will likely change how I "do" church in the years ahead.

One has to wonder whether the church has been more concerned with perpetuating the party line than the vigorous exploration of truth, more committed to propaganda and talking points than the careful examination of our stated beliefs. If there ever were a time when the perceived benefits of unquestioned beliefs were so great people were reluctant to scrutinize the church's claims, it now appears those days are over. The young people I encounter seem increasingly unwilling to grant the church an intellectual pass and are not inclined at all to heed the church's self-declared authority. While some in the church lament this loss of credibility, I believe this skepticism might be helpful, especially if it makes the church more relevant. Such a church would earn our allegiance not by demanding it, but by earning it, by demonstrating its willingness to pursue truth beyond the worn and rutted paths it has traveled in the past.

What would it mean if the church valued questions as much as answers?

In the years following the Second World War, there was a dramatic population shift away from the family farm to urban and suburban areas. This population transfer was fueled, in part, by the GI Bill and the opportunity it provided for returning soldiers to attend college and seek more lucrative employment. When one drives through these farming communities today, it is not unusual to see boarded-up stores, closed churches, and decaying barns and houses.

In some ways, this is similar to witnessing the slow and protracted death of someone we love. A way of life millions of people found meaningful and enriching has come to an end. Nowhere is this more evident than in churches, when one listens to its members recall a church that once teemed with children and young families but is now populated only by senior citizens. Sadly, this decline is sometimes accompanied by a theology that tends to exclude more than include and inflame rather than inspire, often generating more heat than light.

Several years ago, I learned of a growing, vibrant church located in a community that was, in every other respect, dying on the vine. I was eager to visit with its pastor and learn the reason for its renewal. Coincidentally, shortly after learning about this church, I was invited to speak there at an evening Lenten program.

To be honest, I expected their pastor to be strongly evangelistic, to have developed an exciting program for the town's children and youth, and to have invested every waking moment visiting people, inviting them to church. That isn't what I found. While the pastor described herself as an evangelical, she was socially progressive. The church had a youth program, but it was in no way remarkable, and the pastor was only nominally involved. She had invited people to attend church and had worked hard to create a welcoming environment, but many pastors do that with little success. When I asked her about the growth of the church, she seemed somewhat mystified by it, said it had happened at every church she'd ever pastored, that she was grateful for it, but didn't fully understand the reason for it. "I guess I just try to make people feel at home," she told me.

In my evening there, and in subsequent conversations with its members, what I discovered was a pastor who'd helped create such an accepting, open environment that people were attracted to it in droves.

"I can be myself here," one lady told me.

"I don't feel like anyone is judging me," a man said.

Another man told me of going through a difficult period after the death of his wife, of going to the pastor and expressing doubt about God's existence. "It didn't bother her a bit. She told me if her spouse had died, she'd have doubts about God too."

One lady described their adult Sunday-school class. "You can say anything. And I mean anything. Nothing rattles her. She doesn't get upset. If you ask her a question, she takes it seriously. And if you disagree with her, it doesn't bother her. She just listens and smiles and doesn't treat you any differently."

As I got to know the pastor, I discerned she was deeply curious, eager to discuss substantive matters, and not so wedded to her worldview that she couldn't entertain other perspectives. She was well-read, interested in a broad variety of subjects, and immune from our common need to have others agree with us. Because of this, her church became known as a place persons interested in spiritual and intellectual growth could gather. But it was not a coldly cerebral church. Her sense of humor and warm compassion for others infused the community with such joy and verve that all sorts of persons were drawn to it—college graduates, high-school dropouts, rich, poor, evangelical, skeptics, traditional, and progressive. Together, they offered an experience that was relationally, spiritually, and mentally stimulating.

Her church was precisely what I believe the church could be—an engaged and loving community wrestling with the complexities and challenges of life, people who believe their relationship with God should expand their world, not shrink it. While I suspect a pastor's importance in a given congregation is sometimes exaggerated, I do believe this pastor's spiritual tenor was instrumental in this church's growth. Specifically, I believe her intellectual and spiritual curiosity, coupled with her obvious affection for people, helped create a compelling and winsome environment.

It has been said that no good deed goes unpunished. The pastor's district superintendent, who had been uniformly supportive and appreciative of her ministry, retired. He was replaced by a zealot who demanded theological conformity from the pastors in his district. When she refused to be cowed by his bluster and demands, he began working actively to have her transferred from the district. Fortunately, he was not vested with the institutional power to remove her. She continued her work, and her church continued to grow. While his machinations had little effect, I think it outrageous that the one bright flame in his district was a fire he would have happily extinguished.

If the church valued exploration over exhortation, it would actively support those leaders who create seedbeds for our mental and spiritual growth. It would urge pastors to be less concerned with propping up an irrelevant, dogmatic faith and equip them with the necessary tools to help their churches transform lives.

In a friend's denomination, an initiative was undertaken to help fund and foster the spiritual growth of its congregations. One congregation, dying, with less than twenty attendees, was given thousands of dollars to buy a projector to display the words to praise songs on the wall behind the pulpit. Another congregation applied for assistance to send a gifted member to a class in spiritual direction so he would be equipped to help others grow. The committee wrestled with their request for only a short time before telling the church, "That's not what we had in mind when we started this initiative." As my friend told me this story, I thought it an ironic summary of church life today. All manner of support is given to sing the songs of a dying worldview, but scant resources are provided to help others form and articulate a credible and dynamic faith.

In recent years, I was invited to lead a workshop for a hundred pastors in an Eastern state. When I arrived, the denominational official urged me not to say anything that might upset the more staid pastors in the district. Since I had been invited to articulate an intelligible, progressive vision for the church, I was taken aback by his request. The district was populated with highly educated persons who were leaving the denomination in droves. In an effort to stop this hemorrhaging, the denomination had resolved to encourage and equip its clergy to provide more thoughtful, relevant messages. But at the first hint of resistance, the denomination buckled, preferring slow death over new life. It was as if they said, "We would rather retain a view of God many people find meaningless and irrelevant, even if it kills us, than consider a view of the Divine Life that would require us to change or grow."

Conversely, I have been privileged to visit many churches filled to overflowing with people, teeming with life, and making a vital difference in their communities. Invariably, it was the result of courageous leaders, in the pulpit and pew, who had worked prophetically and creatively to overcome the homeostasis of the institutional church. Their efforts were almost always resisted, they were often ostracized for their labors and made to feel less than Christian, even as they endeavored to help their churches become more authentically Christian. Those leaders understood their primary mission was not to administrate a museum, but to create an environment conducive to human growth and transformation.

We who are in the church must get over the notion that our chief duty is to perpetuate it. When our main objective is to propagate an institution, we inevitably limit any questions or observations that challenge its standing. I once attended a debate where the congressman who represented my district told the audience no questions would be permitted. The crowd was well-mannered, but the congressman obviously believed the very act of questioning to be a threat to his political longevity. Instead, he spent his allotted time telling the audience how his views were superior to his rival's. When the moderator posed questions, the congressman was resentful and refused to answer them directly.

During the debate, I was bothered by the man's conduct and recalled another time I had been similarly frustrated. It was when a belligerent church elder had accused someone of trying to split the church when the person questioned a theo-logical doctrine. In both instances, the perpetuation of power was so important that any question was deemed a threat to his authority and the church's longevity.

Until we learn that the chief goal of the church is not its perpetuation, we will continue to resent any questions or activities that might undermine the church's credibility. In that regard, these holders of power were right—honest, open questions will always be a threat to the current order. The present arrangements will have to change, grow, or die. That so many would prefer death over a loss of power is a sad tes-timony to what the church has become and underscores the hard and courageous work required to transform it.

Jesus confronted the attitude of religious superiority preva-lent in his day. In the fifteenth chapter of the gospel of Luke, he told the parables of the lost sheep and the lost coin, chal-lenging his hearer's theological assumptions. The parables are cleverly told, each beginning with a question—"What man of you, having a hundred sheep, if he has lost one of them, does not leave the ninety-nine in the wilderness, and go after the one which is lost until he finds it?" and "What woman, having ten silver coins, if she loses one coin, does not light a lamp and sweep the house and seek diligently until she finds it?"

At first glance, these queries seem innocuous, but they burrow into the conscience, prodding the listener to recon-sider the parameters of God's love. In a religious culture that tended to limit God's affections to the religious insiders,

Jesus's questions revealed a divine fondness for the spiritually estranged. This theme of inclusion was a recurring one in the ministry of Jesus and called into doubt first-century Judaism's presumption of divine favor.

While honest challenges to our settled assumptions can be painful, they can also provoke us to view our world differently. Unfortunately, the reaction of Jesus's audience was less enlightened. Luke tells us "they scoffed at him."[1] This is often the response of the religiously entrenched when urged to reevaluate what they thought were timeless truths. The test of our life in the Spirit is our ability to welcome as good news the very questions that in the end might break us down to build us up.

1. Luke 16:14.

If the Church 6 Were Christian . . .

Encouraging Personal Exploration Would Be More Important Than Communal Uniformity

When I graduated from high school, I was uncertain what I wanted to do with my life and didn't have money to pay for college, so I applied for a job at a regional electric company. I was hired to work in the billing department but was soon promoted to the computer room, where I developed a suspicion of computers that persists to this day. While there, I befriended a man active in Jehovah's Witnesses. Because I was young and spiritually open, I was intrigued with Jehovah's Witnesses and attended church several times with my friend. He was a kind, friendly man, so I was naturally curious about the religion he claimed had made him that way. I was warmly welcomed and invited by those present to return and study the Bible with them.

I was growing increasingly interested in my friend's religion, until one day when he began discussing a situation in their local congregation. A man in the church had divorced his wife and left their denomination. My friend lamented these developments and the loss of his friendship. I was confused by his reaction. "Isn't he still your friend?" I asked.

"Not any longer," my friend said. "We've disfellowshipped him."

I was unfamiliar with that term and asked my friend what it meant. "I can't see or speak to him until he repents and rejoins the church," he explained.

"What if you see him on the street and he says hello to you?" I asked.

"I can't acknowledge him," my friend said.

To say I was shocked would be an understatement. "I know you frown on divorce, but he might have had a good reason for it. And just because he left your church doesn't mean he's a bad person," I pointed out. "Is there no room in your church for forgiveness?"

"Yes, but only if he repents and rejoins the church."

He went on to say that when the man was baptized, he knew their standards of conduct and was well aware of the consequences awaiting those who violated the standards.

My friend's response seemed incongruent with his personality. I sensed he had his own doubts about this practice but felt pressured to participate, lest he also be shunned by his many friends and family in the congregation.

Though I had been giving serious thought to attending church with him, I no longer felt drawn to the Witnesses and decided to become further involved with the Quakers, who seemed more amenable to differences in lifestyle and theology. Ironically, as I began to learn more about the Quakers, I was surprised to hear we'd spent a good portion of the eighteenth and nineteenth centuries disfellowshipping our fellow Friends. We disowned or "read out of meeting" persons who broke any of the innumerable rules of earlier Friends. Included in the list of offenses were marrying outside the Quaker faith, failure to follow the standards of Quaker dress and speech, participation in war, taking part in sacraments, worshipping outside the Quaker community, playing or owning a musical instrument, dancing, drunkenness, spreading hurtful gossip, attending the theater or circus, joining the Masons, taking part in the slave trade, suing a fellow Friend, declaring bankruptcy, or participating in questionable business practices.[1]

While those disowned were permitted to worship with Friends, they were not allowed to participate in the business meetings of the congregation. (Having sat through hundreds of interminably long Quaker business meetings, I fail to see how that could be considered punishment.) Though definitive numbers aren't available, it is estimated that some yearly meetings disfellowshipped a significant number of their members. In a twenty-one year period, from 1755 to 1776, Philadelphia Yearly Meeting disfellowshipped 3,157 of its members, nearly 20 percent of its 15,000 members. By the close of 2007, Philadelphia Yearly Meeting had still not recovered from its loss of membership and had only 11,600 members.[2]

The disfellowshipped Quakers were not excluded from community. Indeed, other Quakers were urged to be kind and gracious to them, in hopes their hearts would be softened, they would repent, and be restored to full fellowship. Unfortunately, most persons read out of meeting didn't feel the love and left the Religious Society of Friends to join other denominations. One of the most common refrains heard by Quakers today is usually voiced by Methodists—"My ancestors were Quakers."

Every summer, my family and I vacation in an area that is home to a large Amish community. We drive past their well-ordered farms, enjoy the food they prepare, and envy the simplicity of their lives. It is easy to forget that these gentle Amish practice a form of shunning that is especially brutal, severing relationships between parents and children, brother and sister, husbands and wives. Because the Amish are isolated from those outside their faith and their economic well-being is directly related to their involvement in the Amish community, this is an especially cruel punishment, effectively condemning the shunned to a life of lonely deprivation.

Shunning seems so far removed from the character of Jesus, one can't help but wonder why certain of his followers embraced this tradition. Nowhere in the Gospels does Jesus advocate this practice. If Jesus had shunned anyone, it likely would have been those who shunned. The apostle Paul was a bit more zealous and advised early Christians to not keep company with fornicators, coveters, idolaters, drunkards, railers, extortionists, and those who cause division (see 1 Corinthians 5:11 and Romans 16:17). Such is the human passion for shunning that we happily sought additional reasons to exclude others. Quakers disfellowshipped persons for adding buttons and collars to their clothing, which we believed were a grievous offense to God.

It should give us pause to remember that Jesus was shunned. At his trial, some of the voices raised loudest against him were those of the leaders of his own tradition, who railed against Jesus because of their penchant for communal uniformity and his tendency to occasionally disregard it. That so many gatekeepers in today's church act in ways Jesus roundly condemned is one of the great ironies of modern Christianity.

I am not without sympathy for our impulse toward proper conduct. Embracing the way of Jesus should transform the way we live. When members of a faith community tarnish a community's credibility and public witness, some form of correction might well be appropriate. But when the corrective is more destructive than the behavior it condemns, something is awry.

Given the zeal with which we ostracize those who are different, one might wonder if the drive for communal uniformity is less motivated by our passion for moral purity and more symptomatic of an obsession with control. I once watched a televangelist being interviewed about a college he'd begun for aspiring preachers. The interview showed students in a homiletics class, most of whom bore an uncanny resemblance to the televangelist. They had not only adopted his theology, which was likely a prerequisite for admittance, but they had also assumed his mannerisms, speech patterns, and attire. When I was in seminary, I had the good fortune of hearing the great preacher Fred Craddock speak. For the next several months, my sermons were vain efforts to sound just like him. While mimicking those we admire isn't uncommon, it's another matter entirely when emulation is required and rewarded.

While communal uniformity might help assimilate people into a fellowship, it too often reduces people to mindless imitators, ultimately robbing the community of the intellectual vitality and diversity it needs to grow and evolve. Churches primarily concerned with communal uniformity encourage spiritual inbreeding, where theological DNA is replicated over and over, fostering spiritual deformity. This might be the greatest danger of communal uniformity—it discourages, if not outright forbids, the progression of a healthy faith. It freezes a community in a given moment, insists it has reached the pinnacle of understanding, and thwarts any effort to move the group forward. Advocates of conformity customarily ignore or silence any voice that calls for change.

Several years ago, I attended a church meeting where the topic of homosexuality was being discussed. The man in charge of moderating the dialogue began the meeting by saying, "We're here today to talk about homosexuality, even though we all know it's wrong." Time and again, he recognized only those speakers he knew shared his sentiments. He then called on a woman he believed agreed with him, though it became obvious when the woman began to speak that she'd had a change of heart. The moderator interrupted the woman to announce it was time for lunch. The rest of the day, when anyone urged tolerance and understanding, the moderator would call for a break or simply cut the speaker off and recognize someone else. Curiously, the participants did not grow angry with the moderator's heavy-handedness but instead turned their ire upon those few persons urging the church to be gracious. At mealtime, their efforts to mix and mingle went unreturned, and they sat alone. When they spoke, people groaned and commented loudly, and often rudely, about their remarks.

A few days later, I spoke privately with the moderator, expressing my concern about his conduct. I did not criticize his perspective, which he had every right to hold, but only the manner in which he had used his power to silence alternative voices. I spoke respectfully and softly, with a smile on my face. His reaction was strong and immediate. "If you don't like it, you should leave the church. You're not one of us anyway."

That I had participated in the church all my life and had attended college and graduate school for many years to better understand the church's history and teachings counted for little. The impulse toward communal uniformity was so strong that my sympathy for those trying to move the church in a more enlightened direction apparently disqualified me from participation in the church.

Thus it has always been. Communal uniformity became a priority of the church shortly after the death of Jesus. While Jesus's disciples were initially a disparate lot, they unified quickly enough to hold a conference in Jerusalem to discern whether Gentile Christians should observe the Jewish rituals. Time and again, when faced with the choice between oppressive conformity and personal exploration, the church has opted for uniformity. The consequences of this tendency are so dramatic as to be breathtaking. Today, the church is hemorrhaging members, as more and more thoughtful people look outside the church for enlightenment. Efforts to stem this flight are usually superficial, changing the church's outward appearance but remaining inwardly the same, wedded to a worldview many have found unhelpful in their search for meaning. Though more and more people seem interested in spirituality, they look less and less to the church as a setting for their search.

What if the church began to understand itself as a seedbed of inquiry, as a place where persons could gather to consider what it means to be human? What if the church understood itself less as the conveyor of an unchangeable truth and more as a community of seekers, eager to think, grow, and explore?

What would it mean if the church valued personal exploration over communal uniformity?

One of my earliest memories of church is when I was around eight years old and attending a Catholic church with my family. Our priest, a stolid, unimaginative man, was gone one Sunday, and in his place was a new priest, sent by the diocesan headquarters to perform the Mass for our small parish. This priest was more demonstrative and passionate than our regular priest and captured my attention from his very first words. During his message, he asked a rhetorical question. A child in the congregation, thinking the priest wanted his question answered, yelled it out. The priest began to laugh, and the congregation joined with him.

It stands out in my memory for two reasons—it was the first time I'd heard laughter in church and the first time I'd heard anyone but a priest speak during Mass. It was my first inkling that church could be joyful and participatory. The next Sunday, my mother didn't have to coax me to attend. For the first time ever, I wanted to go to church. But when we arrived, our regular priest had returned home, the new priest was gone, and it seemed to me a palpable gloom had settled over the sanctuary.

When I became a Quaker, the aspect of church life that most fascinated me was the open worship, when anyone in the congregation who felt led by the Spirit could stand and speak. Over the next several years, as I visited different Quaker meetings, I was surprised to hear persons stand after the pastor had spoken[3] and supplement his or her remarks. Occasionally, the individual would even gently disagree with the pastor and invite the congregation to consider the matter from another perspective. The pastors seemed to take this in stride, I never sensed any animosity, and the gathered congregation was under no compulsion to affirm a particular theology. Sadly, as the theological complexion of Midwestern Quakerism changed, fueled by the rise of evangelical Christianity in the United States, the open, seeking environment I'd found in Quaker meetings began to dim.

But for the first time, I felt as if I'd had a hand in determining my theological worldview, that it would not be imposed on me by someone in authority, that I was encouraged to listen carefully, read widely, and discern the truth for myself. This process was enhanced by thoughtful persons in the church who never dismissed my views, shallow and imprecise as they were at the time. Instead, I was directed to books, teachers, and more seasoned Friends who helped fill the many holes in my knowledge. The environment was one of spiritual curiosity, theological flexibility, and gracious give-and-take. It instilled in me a desire to learn all I could about God, myself, and others.

I have wished many times that that experience could be replicated in churches around the world. Since that time, I've tried to isolate the components that made those settings such spiritually fertile ones. The pastors seemed unthreatened by views different from their own. Interestingly, these pastors were not towering intellects, nor were they theologically sophisticated. But they were comfortable in their own skins, did not need others to affirm their choices in order to feel good about themselves, and consequently seemed very much at home in diverse congregations. Because congregations often take their emotional cues from their leaders, the nonanxious approach of the "head" had a calming effect on the "body."

Unfortunately, I didn't keep these qualities in mind when I first began pastoring. I believed my success hinged on my ability to inspire the congregation to think like me. Naturally, many in the congregations didn't aspire to that, but I resisted their resistance and became doctrinaire. As you can imagine, my tenures were short. I entered my third church tired and discouraged, lacking the strength to hold the reins of leadership as tightly as I had. Providentially, it was only by "letting go" that I began to understand ministry, and life, in a new way. Freer to be myself, and let others be themselves, I discovered my life in the church was no longer exhausting but refreshing. I also discovered that as I loosened my grip on the steering wheel, others were able to steer in directions that better suited their gifts, temperaments, and personalities.

There is an old saying that when the student is ready, the teacher appears. At the same time I was loosening the reins, I began visiting a retired minister, Errol, who belonged to my meeting. Well into his nineties, Errol lived at a retirement center not far from our meetinghouse. He was hard of hearing, so two-way conversation was difficult. Fortunately, he had a lot to say, and I was happy to listen. Each time we visited, he would focus on a particular aspect of church life. Despite his age, he was quite creative, had continued to read and reflect, and was often more cutting edge than many of the younger pastors with whom I normally associated.

One afternoon he said something that has remained with me ever since. "Philip, most pastors teach their congregations *what* to think. We need to teach people *how* to think." He spoke about his spiritual journey, how he'd grown up in a religiously rigid environment where Christianity meant giving one's assent to propositions, whether they made sense or not, whether one understood them or not. Then he became a pastor and observed that the emphasis on content over process had crippled the church's capacity for spiritual reflection and growth. As he began equipping his congregations to think theologically, the churches began to grow, filling with persons eager for a thoughtful, dynamic faith. I've had the good fortune to know a congregation he'd pastored fifty years before—First Friends Meeting in Indianapolis. These many years later, it remains a vital, engaging community, still very much enlivened by the tone he set long ago.

On one visit, Errol gave me a compilation of messages he'd delivered. Reading through them, I was struck time and again by the freshness of his thinking. Though many of them had been written half a century before, his insights leaped off the page. Not content to simply repackage outdated beliefs, he took faith in directions and dimensions I'd never before considered. As I read them, I began to understand God, Jesus, and humanity in a new way. Because Errol's reputation was so stellar, I began to see that the church, at least some elements of it, could honor and appreciate free thinking. It then occurred to me that if free thinking were an admirable quality for clergy, the church could likewise be strengthened when its members felt a similar freedom to explore the "far country" of thought.

Inspired by Errol's example, I changed my approach to ministry. I no longer suggested that by virtue of my theological education I was the resident expert on all matters spiritual. To facilitate this change, I developed a lighter, more playful approach to church life, in which I freely revealed my own struggles and shortcomings, often in a lighthearted way. This had two effects—it softened the dead-serious atmosphere that often accompanies religion, and it reminded the congregation (and me) that I was not exempt from doubts and struggles. I also learned to say, "I don't know," and, "I'm not sure," and I discovered my admitted ignorance about a particular matter often had a galvanizing effect, inspiring others to think for themselves, or read and reflect more deeply on the subject at hand.

To be sure, there were always persons in the congregations who attended church precisely because they valued conformity and certainty. As the church's priorities shifted from communal uniformity to personal exploration, they either left, deeply frustrated by the congregation's unwillingness to be the kind of church they wanted it to be, or they stayed, assumed responsibility for their spiritual formation, and evolved. Unfortunately, the former were more common than the latter, and those who left quickly found other churches whose understanding of God compelled them to limit and restrict others.

I found in Jesus this same passion for spiritual exploration. In the fifth, sixth, and seventh chapters of Matthew are found a collection of teachings commonly referred to as the Sermon on the Mount. As a child, I was told Jesus had ascended a mountain to deliver a lengthy message that was later recorded in Matthew's gospel. Later, I learned mountaintops were considered places of divine revelation and that Matthew used that setting to portray Jesus as a new lawgiver, a new Moses.[4] I also learned that the Sermon on the Mount had probably never been given in its entirety, but was the collected sayings of Jesus assembled into one piece.

However one interprets that event, it is clear that those Jesus sayings assumed a central role in the life of the church. At the core of these teachings is found a back-and-forth rhythm of old revelation and new revelation. Jesus would begin by saying, "You have heard that it was said . . ." Then he would say, "But I say to you . . . ," offering a new teaching, a fresh perspective. I imagine some of Jesus's hearers were scandalized by the apparent freedom he felt to move beyond a time-honored teaching in order to emphasize a greater truth. Were communal uniformity a priority for Jesus, he would never have felt liberated to suggest another way of living.

In the gospel of Luke,[5] Jesus asked his disciples what others were saying about him. They offered a variety of answers. Then Jesus asked, "Who do you say that I am?" In the past, I assumed that was a pass-or-fail question, a test Jesus gave to judge his disciple's orthodoxy. I suspect this has been the common interpretation of that text. But think how uncharacteristic that would have been for Jesus, whose regard for orthodoxy was never all that keen. Jesus, never one to make thus-sayeth-the-Lord pronouncements, taught through the use of stories, parables, and questions, letting his hearers arrive at some great truth at their own pace. Think for a moment how many of his most memorable teachings centered on a question:

You are the salt of the earth; but if salt has lost its taste, how shall its saltness be restored?[6]

Is not life more than food, and the body more than clothing?[7]

Why do you see the speck that is in your brother's eye, but do not notice the log that is in your own eye?[8]

Religious institutions committed to communal uniformity seldom ask questions. The risk of straying beyond conventional answers is too great. Jesus asked questions because he believed in their power to engage his hearers, and he wanted his disciples to consider the reality of God in other ways, not regurgitate past platitudes that had lost their meaning and vigor. His frequent encouragement for others to embrace a new manner of being reveals a man quite comfortable with independent thought and action, who urged his hearers to flourish and grow and not be spiritually root-bound. In asking his disciples, "Who do you say that I am?" Jesus was inviting them to reconsider what they believed about God and how God was present in the world.

Perhaps the most important task of a spiritual guide is to help create a community where people can safely reevaluate their beliefs. Persons occasionally speak to me about feeling spiritually "stuck." More often than not, they have hailed from traditions whose religious explorations were limited to a strict and literal interpretation of the Bible. While that theology had an initial appeal, it often didn't hold up to the complexities of life, and they became disillusioned, no longer believing that the church, or at least the church they'd experienced, was an effective partner in spiritual formation. Their response is almost always predictable and will take one of two forms: They leave the church, convinced it has little to offer (unfortunately, this is the most common reaction). Or sometimes they discover a community whose understanding of faith is broader and richer than they've experienced, a community where exploration is valued over conformity.

Because questions help our spiritual evolution, early Quakers devised a series of queries, encouraging their regular and frequent consideration as an aid in our spiritual formation. I have participated in worship groups whose focus on these questions led to transformative insights, often taking me in directions I hadn't anticipated. I have seen this happen time and again with others. Having hungered for such a community, our joy in finding such places is so infectious that even as we are blessed by the community, we enrich it in return. This to me is the church at its best, uniting in love and learning, but not so slavishly committed to uniformity that our responsibility for personal exploration is lost.

1. There is an uneven quality to these restrictions. It is likely God is more disappointed with slavery than piano playing.
2. This information was supplied to me by Thomas Hamm, archivist and professor of history of Earlham College in Richmond, Indiana. For further information about this and other Quaker matters, you can read Tom's fine book, *The Transformation of American Quakerism*, published by Indiana University Press in 1988. The statistic about Philadelphia Yearly Meeting's current membership was provided by Arthur M. Larrabee, the general secretary of Philadelphia Yearly Meeting.
3. All the Quaker meetings I attended were programmed meetings, which employed pastors. Other Quaker congregations are unprogrammed and do not employ paid pastoral leadership. The geographic location and theological history of a meeting has much to do with whether a Quaker meeting is programmed or unprogrammed.
4. Interestingly, Luke collected many of the same teachings but changed the setting to "a level place." Were I a fundamentalist, I would be troubled by this incongruity.
5. Luke 9:18–20.
6. Matthew 5:13.
7. Matthew 6:25.
8. Matthew 7:3.

If the Church Were Christian . . .

Meeting Needs Would Be More Important
Than Maintaining Institutions

During and after seminary, I pastored a small Quaker meeting in the city of Indianapolis. Like many neighborhoods in the city, ours was economically mixed. People on food stamps lived only a few blocks from millionaires. Because of their proximity, the comfortable and poor intermingled at the neighborhood park, shopped in the same grocery stores, and attended the same churches. Hardly a day passed that someone wouldn't phone my office or stop by the meetinghouse for assistance. Our meeting was a small one—less than two dozen people my first year there—but eager to provide whatever help we could to persons in need.

One of the local congregations had a food pantry but claimed to be chronically short of food donations. Because it had been established for some time and was known to persons in need, we decided that assisting that pantry rather than starting our own made more sense. The first week of our venture, I transported the food our members had donated to the food pantry and stayed to help distribute the items. Oddly, the pantry was only open once a week, for one hour, in the early afternoon, when most people were at work.

Two women from the host church were overseeing the process. They opened the doors precisely at one o'clock, handed out a few cans of vegetables to each family, then closed the doors one hour later, to the minute, even though another family, who had walked some distance to get there, hadn't yet been helped.

"Come back next week," one of the women told them.

I was taken aback by her actions, but since it was my first time to help, I was reluctant to argue. Instead, I began helping the women put away the food that hadn't been given out. When I entered the pantry storeroom, I was amazed to see cartons of food stacked on shelves and pallets on the floor.

"My gosh," I said. "There's enough food here to feed the entire city. Why did we give people so little when we had so much?"

"We don't want to give away all our food," one of the women said.

"But when people donate to a food pantry, don't you think they want to see it handed out instead of sitting in a church basement somewhere?" I asked. "What good is it doing anyone down here?"

Neither of them responded.

I returned the next three weeks. As I worked alongside the women, it became evident that instead of distributing food, they were doing all they could not to give it away—limiting the hours of distribution, putting such rigid conditions in place that fewer and fewer families qualified for assistance, and changing the weekly hours of operation with little or no advance notice to those in need.

Not long afterward, I crossed paths with another member of their church, who asked my perception of their food pantry.

"I have never seen two people work so hard to do so little," I told him.

"Yeah, it's a mess," he said. "We never should have put them in charge of it. Now we can't get it away from them. They're dug in, and it'd be too big a battle to get them out."

I almost said, "I wouldn't let that happen in a church I pastored," but caught myself in time, recalling moments I had let institutional functions (and dysfunctions) trump the church's mission and purpose. Indeed, I remembered instances where my own inclination toward institutionalism had caused me to neglect the needs of others. This might be a universal given with any institution—every organization inevitably forgets the values that inspired its start and focuses instead on its own perpetuation.

In a speech to the Whitsitt Society in 1995, the Southern Baptist preacher and prophet Will D. Campbell spoke about his checkered history with religious institutions. "I was a pastor, a university chaplain, an employee of the allegedly most free religious institution in the world. I didn't keep any job for long. But through it all I discovered one thing. All institutions, every last single one of them, are evil; self-serving, self-preserving, self-loving; and very early in the life of any institution it will exist for its own self."[1]

Several times a year, I receive a letter from someone chiding me for leaving the Roman Catholic Church. While I am grateful for my religious heritage, my decision to leave Catholicism was made over thirty years ago and isn't one I'm likely to revisit. The letters are consistent in theme—the Roman Church is the true church, is institutionally pure, and is the only way to God. These beliefs require such a wholesale suspension of reality that I scarcely know how to respond to them. It is like arguing with someone from the Flat Earth Society.

Anyone who believes in the institutional purity of any church has not been deeply and thoughtfully involved with organized religion. It is only possible to maintain the delusion of institutional purity by remaining willfully ignorant of the many ways religions have forsaken their core values. This delusion transcends denominational boundaries. I have met Quakers who earnestly believe the Religious Society of Friends is exempt from the moral compromises that challenge every other human institution. I remember staring, dumbfounded, as a woman told me that in all her years as a

Quaker she had never seen her fellow Friends do the wrong thing. It reminded me of those parents who swore their little Johnny would never say a bad word.

This blindness to the institutional failings of the church causes irreparable harm, perhaps as much or more harm than the failings themselves. For until we are mindful of the church's failures, we'll do nothing to mend them. Unfortunately, it seems to be a common trait among humans and the institutions we create to ignore our flaws even as those failings cripple our ability to function and grow. For too long, the church has been a bit like the alcoholic who continues to insist he doesn't have a problem. Everyone in the room can see the problem except the one who has it.

This blindness is perpetuated when the church insists it is not a human institution, prone to error, but a divine institution and therefore infallible. What a divorce from reality this assertion requires! It not only ignores the very human origins of the church, it conveniently overlooks the emotional and sexual abuse, wars, infighting, greed, racism, and sexism in which the church participates. Still, the myth of the church's purity is a potent one, and one we are loathe to surrender. It took the prophetic words of Will Campbell to open my eyes, and I suspect I'm still blind to the various ways the church has abandoned its ideals in order to perpetuate its power and presence, and I'm even blind to my own collaboration.

I have caught myself urging my congregations to do what was best for our institutional longevity with little regard for

ing values. How ironic, when one considers that
ss to those values—feeding the hungry, befriend-
nely, loving the enemy, healing the sick, visiting the
prisoners, helping others know the Divine Presence—would
do more to ensure the church's well-being than the most
astute planning. The same ministries that would save our
ecclesial lives and bring vibrancy to our religious institutions
are the very things Jesus told us to do. They would have an
inspiring effect, multiplying the feelings of goodwill, usefulness, and effectiveness every organization requires for its
long-term health. In my quarter century of church leadership,
I have never, not once, seen a church wither whose members
were active in ministry. Instead, time and again I have seen
churches revived and persons renewed when they were motivated and inspired to love widely and care deeply for those
around them. It is so simple a truth that it seems formulaic,
but it is as true a law as gravity—in helping others, we help
ourselves.

Our resistance to this simple truth boggles the mind. In my
own denomination, the Society of Friends, I have participated
in regional gatherings where assets of millions of dollars were
reported and celebrated, while requests for modest assistance
to the needy were debated at length. Then, with little awareness of the rich irony, we wondered aloud why our numbers
were dwindling and our institutions faltering. I don't for a
moment believe Jesus intended to start a new religious institution. But I do believe the principles he articulated, summa-

rized in the Sermon on the Mount, would greatly enliven the institution that arose from his life and witness.

What would the church look like if meeting human needs were more important than maintaining institutions?

An acquaintance of mine began attending a small congregation on the outskirts of a large city. The church had its roots in the agricultural community, but the city had grown out to meet it, displacing many of the farm families that had once filled its pews. Like many small churches it struggled financially, but over the years, because of their frugality, the church members had managed to set aside thousands of dollars in an emergency fund. As is often the case, they had grown accustomed to having the money, felt a certain reassurance knowing it was there, and couldn't imagine any circumstance, emergency or otherwise, that would compel them to spend it. The bank balance was reported each month at the church's business meeting; they marveled at its growth and resisted mightily any suggestion to use even a small portion of it in ministry.

As my friend grew more actively involved in the church's life, she began gently questioning their pattern of hoarding. At first people were resistant to her suggestions that they give the money away, but as they got to know her and trust her discernment, they began responding more generously to the needs around them. Within a few years, they had given away most of the money they'd gathered. Though several in the congregation had warned the church would go broke, giving to the church increased.

One man summarized well the feelings of many: "I never gave much before because I knew that money would sit in a bank account, not doing anybody any good. When I saw we were putting it to good use, I wanted to give more."

Of course, our giving shouldn't be motivated by a desire to receive more. But generosity begets generosity. Once that pattern is established, it grows in other dimensions. In this congregation, their expanded outlook caused them to look beyond themselves. They had been inward looking, caring mostly about themselves, blind to anything or anyone beyond their doors. For years, they had failed to attract any new attendees. (I'd often wondered why my friend had chosen to participate in that community.) But as they opened their hearts, they simultaneously opened their doors. They began inviting others to share in their community, and they relinquished their iron grip on power even as they relinquished their grip on their money. New persons were assimilated into the congregation's life, and within a few years they had another problem—what to do with all the people who'd joined their fellowship. Time and again, I have observed the irresistible nature of generous churches. In a world where stingy, narrow religions abound, a big-hearted fellowship has a real allure, especially to persons who've been bruised by bad religion, which is to say, all of us.

A significant barrier to church growth is the understandable cynicism of people who believe the church has lost its way. Having witnessed the church's limited vision, they no longer believe the church can be a transforming community. I have talked with scores, if not hundreds, of these people. Curiously, they are not usually angry at the church. Rather, they are saddened by the church's failure to live up to its ideals. I remember a woman once telling me, "The church breaks my heart. I so want to find one that will make a difference in my life and in the lives of others. But they all end up caring more about themselves than they do others." She was not angry, nor were her words harshly spoken. She was resigned to what appears to be a common reality in most churches—that after a while they exist largely for themselves.

I suspect one reason I've stayed in the church is that my expectations for the church have not been all that high. I have assumed the church will often do the wrong thing, will occasionally get something right, and will in rare circumstances do something so transcendently beautiful that the power and memory of it will sustain me for years.

Those transcendent moments have always involved the church's reaching out to persons in deep pain. I have pastored my current meeting, Fairfield Friends Meeting near Indianapolis, since 1999. Long before my arrival on its shores, this meeting had cultivated a habit of kindness. These mercies were exercised quietly, never publicly or even formally through the meeting's committee structures, though those structures had a knack for doing good.

Unaware of their compassion, I thought it my job to teach them that trait, but I came to realize they were teaching me. I would visit someone in the hospital only to learn others had been there before me. I would hear of a material need and go to meet it, only to find someone had been there before me with money, food, or assistance. I heard stories of alcoholics befriended by the meeting, restored to health, and given employment. In my years there, I have seen homes opened to the homeless, money raised for the poor, food given to the hungry, the lonely befriended, and mercy shown to the despised.

I know my church is not an anomaly, that there are many others like it. I also know even the best churches can be easily sidetracked by a small number of persons whose priorities are skewed. In one of the first churches I pastored, we met to decide how best to help a family down on their luck, through no fault of their own. Just as consensus was building to respond generously and creatively to their need, a man rose to his feet and began complaining about the money it would cost. The church had ample funds, but this man had appointed himself the unofficial guardian of the congregation's resources and actively fought every expenditure outside the budget.

"The church is like any other business," he said. "We've got to stick to our budget."

A brave soul pointed out that the church was not a business and that we had sufficient funds to meet our budget and help the family. But I could tell that the old bromide about "the church as a business" had struck a chord with some members and their desire to help one of our own was fading in the face of this man's objection.

I stood and spoke. "Moments like these are important," I said. "Now we get to decide what kind of church we're going to be. Are we going to care more about people or more about our bottom line?"

I hadn't been there long enough for my words to carry any weight, and within a few minutes it was decided to forward the matter to a committee, which in that church was the kiss of death. Unfortunately, it served to reinforce a pattern of stinginess in that congregation and decades later they've not been able to shake it. They do little for one another or anyone else, expend all their energies propping up their tired institution, and barely fill a third of their empty, yawning meetinghouse.

Despite this, I have hope for that church, as I do for every church. I believe their pattern of indifference can be undone in one moment, with one decision to reach beyond them-selves. That congregation will gather to discuss their busi-ness, a need will be presented, and they will proceed down their same tired road of indifference, but then someone will say, "Hold on. Why are we here if not to minister to people? Let's reconsider." And because goodness has a contagious effect, another person will add her voice, then another, and their chain of apathy will be broken. This seems to me to be an inviolate truth—maintaining the necessary enthusiasm to prop up a tired institution is very difficult, and we eventually weary of it, but doing good has a regenerative effect, inspiring us to work hard, give generously, and think creatively.

Nevertheless, it is profoundly difficult to challenge the status quo in most churches. Many of the people advocating institutional maintenance over human need are those who hold power in the congregation. Sometimes that power is formal, allowing them to direct the considerable resources of the church toward institutional maintenance. But just as often their power is informal and exercised behind the scenes, as they quietly sabotage any effort to help those outside the church. In most churches, it makes very little difference who is appointed to lead, which is why efforts to change the ethos of a congregation through the proper chain of command can be so frustrating. Many a pastor has tried to fill a board with persons sympathetic to outreach and human need only to find it made little practical difference in the church's focus and ministry. This, more than long hours and low pay, might be the reason pastoral tenure is trending downward.

Perhaps the most frustrating moment in a pastor's life is when he or she realizes that no matter how thoughtful, eloquent, or biblically sound a sermon, it will not move an entrenched congregation in a new direction overnight. Indeed, sometimes entire years will pass with no discernable shift in a congregation's priorities. Congregations are like people; unless they are in a crisis, they change their patterns and habits slowly. This is a good argument for pastoral longevity. It often takes sustained, creative leadership to alter long-established patterns in the church. Unfortunately, many pastors are either fired or leave of their own accord just as they're about to become effective.

When I first became a pastor, I tended to demonize persons who resisted my efforts to shift the congregation's priorities. I believed their rejection of my concerns was symptomatic of an unhealthy spirituality, that they were in need of correction, and that I was the one God had appointed to fix them. But as I got to know these persons, I realized their motives for institutional maintenance were more noble than I had thought. They sincerely believed institutional maintenance was the proper work and calling of the church. They did what they did because they thought God wanted them to. They had simply forgotten the institutional church was a means, not the end.

Looking after a building and maintaining the necessary financial and committee structures is important, but only to the extent they contribute to the church's primary mission of seeking transformation and meeting human need. What made Fairfield Meeting such an engaged, involved congregation was their habit, at key moments in their corporate life, of remembering why they were there. This was helped by their habit of granting formal and informal power to persons we Quakers call "weighty" Friends. These are people who, because of their wisdom, spiritual maturity, and gracious temperament, are sought out for counsel and direction. Fairfield was (and is) blessed to have a considerable number of such persons who skillfully and faithfully motivated the congregation to heed its better angels.

I suspect there are people like that in each congregation. The trick is in making sure those voices are heard above the myriad voices that would distract us from our mission. Too often, those who are more strident drown out the softer voices of wiser saints. I've often thought the most important job of the pastor is making sure those gentler voices are heard and heeded.

In one of my former churches there was a woman named Denise who was very wise, but reserved. Not one to speak off the top of her head, she preferred to let ideas season before sharing her perspective. On several occasions, I found myself urging the congregation to not hastily settle a matter until we'd given ourselves ample time to consider the issue more deliberately. A few days later, I would phone or visit Denise to pick her brains. Often, her insight not only improved upon anything we had considered, it called us back to our mission. As I got to know Denise, I learned she had spent part of her life serving as a nurse in the African nation of Liberia. That experience informed her understanding of God and flavored her vision of what the church should be. Few persons in the meeting knew Denise's background of compassionate ministry. She never presumed that experience gave her a moral or spiritual authority, though it was clear it had given her an understanding and passion for ministry. In time, the meeting recognized that gift and invited her to leadership. Because of her demure personality, leadership did not always come easily to her, but she handled the responsibility well, having a profound effect on the meeting and its priorities.

My experience with Denise caused me to think more carefully about the types of personalities we invite to leadership in the church and how those personalities affect the church's direction and focus. A friend of mine and fellow minister was invited to pastor an affluent congregation in the South. He was especially delighted because the congregation had a number of successful businesspersons who were eager to lend their expertise to the church.

A year or so into his ministry, I met my friend for lunch. He began talking about his church and seemed somewhat discouraged. "They're very nice people," he said. "Very efficient. They keep the place up. And they're well organized."

As we discussed his situation, he observed the church's leadership was comprised solely of businesspeople, all of whom were bright and gifted. They had done a masterful job of organizing and streamlining the church's committee structure, had enhanced the church's physical appearance, and vastly improved the church's financial arrangements. "It feels like we're a Fortune 500 company," my friend said. "It's incredible. But I don't know that we're doing anyone any good."

I thought of all the times I had struggled with inefficiency and disorganization in the congregations I'd pastored and offered to take a few of his congregants off his hands.

"The thing with a lot of businesspeople," he said, "is that they look at every situation through the eyes of business and every solution is a business solution. You know what they say: when all you have is a hammer, every problem is a nail."

We continued to meet for lunch a couple of times a year. "Well," he told me during one of our visits, "we're starting to shake things up."

"What did you do?"

"Got a social worker, teacher, and nurse appointed to the board," he said. "They're driving the businesspeople crazy. They started a child-care center for poor kids. Hired a director, cleaned up some rooms, organized volunteers, then told the businesspeople God would supply the money. You ever want to drive businesspeople nuts, tell them God will pay for something." He started laughing. "They asked the social worker what her business plan was for the child-care center."

Then he turned serious. "The trick," he said, "will be in finding the balance. We need these business folk. They're really savvy. But we need the 'people' people too. They remind us why we're here."

That was as fine a summation as I've ever heard on the importance of balanced leadership. My own congregation is gifted with many talented businesspeople and entrepreneurs. They have a knack for organization, fiscal discipline, and thoughtful management. Our congregation would be in real jeopardy without them. Fortunately, their institutional prowess is complemented by social workers, teachers, nurses, doctors, and others in the helping professions, whose passion for hands-on ministry reminds us of the church's calling.

Though the apostle Paul couldn't have foretold the complexity of the modern church, he did recognize the benefits of diverse gifts and their usefulness in achieving a good end. "There are," he wrote, "varieties of gifts, but the same Spirit; and varieties of service, but the same Lord . . . [all working together] for the common good."[2]

At the end of the day, it is important to remember that while the institutional church is important to us, Jesus appeared to give it little thought. Though the church eventually became the means by which the story and witness of Jesus spread, neither its genesis nor continuance seemed a priority to him. Time after time, meeting human needs took center stage in his life and ministry. Indeed, when Jesus did speak of institutional religion, he was often scathing, saying at one point that those who were religiously pure on the outside were inwardly deceitful and rapacious.[3] This serves as a caution to those of us who've convinced ourselves that the goal of the church is institutional purity. To be a follower of Jesus is to choose, at every ethical crossroads, to serve people above structures.

1. Excerpted from Campbell's speech, "A Personal Struggle for Soul Freedom," which I discovered on the Web site of *Christian Ethics Today: Journal of Christian Ethics.* You can visit that Web site at www.christianethicstoday.com.

2. See Paul's comments on the benefits of diversity in the twelfth chapter of his first letter to the Corinthians.

3. Matthew 23:25.

If the Church Were Christian . . .

Peace Would Be More Important Than Power

While in my early twenties, I began developing an interest in ministry. Though working at a large public utility, I spent much of my spare time volunteering at a Quaker meeting near my home. I found the work interesting and fulfilling, began taking night classes in Bible, sociology, and theology, and, encouraged by others in the meeting, I made plans to quit my job, enroll in college, and prepare for pastoral ministry. Before quitting my job, I visited my parents to tell them my plans. My father had not made the church part of his life but was receptive to the idea. My mother, who had been active in the church since childhood and had even been employed as the principal of a Catholic school, urged me to consider another vocation. She did so graciously, expressing concern that I would fall victim to the power and politics of organized religion and become cynical. Though I was not aware of it at the time, that had been the consequence of her participation in the church.

While I respected my mother, I did not heed her advice and proceeded with my plans. Though I have not regretted that decision, I now understand her concern. Perhaps no day is so sobering as when one's innocence is first wounded. I remember the day my belief in the purity of the church was tested. I had been working with the youth of the church. When I told the church elders of my leading to become a pastor, they formalized my work with the youth by giving me the title "intern pastor" and paying me a small stipend. As part of my duties, I was required to attend the monthly elders' meeting. There were eight elders in the congregation, ostensibly chosen for their wisdom and spiritual maturity. Indeed, most of the elders were deeply committed to the church's mission and served that role creatively and faithfully. But one of the elders had clear designs on power. She bullied and intimidated the other elders, manipulating the Quaker process of discernment to get her way. The head elder was a passive man, lacking the courage to address inappropriate behavior. I left that first meeting troubled and somewhat disillusioned.

That evening I lay awake reflecting on the meeting and the elder's conduct. I wondered what she had to gain by her grab for power. There was no financial benefit to be had. The Quaker meeting was a relatively small one, certainly not the most prestigious church in town, so there was little prominence attached to the elders' role. In truth, most of the elders probably served reluctantly, out of a sense of obligation or affection toward the church. But I had the sense that if the church had asked for volunteers, that elder would have been the first to raise her hand and, if not selected, would nevertheless have found a way to maneuver herself onto that committee.

This might have been my first deep awareness of the appeal of power and how, even when confined to a small community, power held a special attraction for some people. The elder's lust for power was not a secret; others in the meeting spoke about it, often voicing their frustration. But the church as a whole seemed ill-equipped to deal with her self-absorbed behavior. As a young minister, I found her intimidating and made sure to fly under her radar, dismissing her behavior as misguided, but essentially harmless.

Unfortunately, the abuse of power is anything but harmless. Over the next several years, I watched as that elder generated such ill will in the congregation that people left rather than endure spiritual and emotional maltreatment. In almost every church I have been associated with, I have seen this pattern. A small minority of persons long for power and control, and others react passively, preferring an accommodating peace over appropriate confrontation, such that the church's ability to progress and grow is stymied. Eventually, healthy persons come to view the church as spiritually and ethically injurious and leave. If they remain, they become, as my mother predicted, cynical and even contemptuous of organized religion.

Not only does abusive power harm the spiritual well-being of its targets, it has a detrimental effect on those who wield it. A hunger for power diminishes our capacity for appropriate humility, crippling our self-awareness, thereby making transformation all the more difficult and unlikely. Time and again, I have seen how those bent on power lack the one quality necessary for their spiritual growth—the ability to assess their spiritual condition honestly so that transformation can take root and grow.

On one occasion, I knew a pastor who'd been appointed to a position of greater leadership. His appointment concerned me, because I sensed he had a fondness for power and control. What was also clear were his gifts for ministry. He was a compelling speaker, possessed much energy, and seemed to genuinely care about Christ and the church. His first months in office went well, and my concerns about him began to ebb. Then a theological matter arose, requiring that he meet with the committee that had oversight of the region's spiritual care. He argued for one course of action, while the members of the committee felt led to take another. They voiced appreciation for his perspective but nevertheless believed a different approach was in order. His reaction was strong and immediate. He refused to comply with their suggestion and demanded they follow his counsel. The committee, taken aback by the force of his response, buckled. As the drama unfolded in the next several months, it was clear that their decision was ruinous and hurtful. It was also clear that the leader would not admit it and was as determined as ever to get his way, even at the expense of the church. When he met with the committee again, he said, "I don't care if only two people remain in the church. We must do this." The intensity of his response was far out of proportion to the original issue, but by then he'd lost all sense of perspective. What was at stake now was his power and his need to have it affirmed.

Shortly afterward, a man in my church handed me a copy of a lecture given by a Catholic monk named Brother David Steindl-Rast. Brother David lived in a monastery in Elmira, New York, had sought permission to practice Zen Buddhism, and through that experience gained many insights. The lecture he gave was titled "The Spiritual Challenge of Joseph Campbell"[1] and was delivered at the Georgetown Center for Liturgy, Spirituality and the Arts.[2]

In that lecture, Brother David spoke about the difference between authority and authoritarianism. He did so by reminding his listeners of the original meaning of the word *authority*, which was defined as someone who possessed "a firm basis of knowing and acting." By way of example, he mentioned that when we're sick, we visit a doctor who is an *authority* on a particular illness. Because of the doctor's expertise, we grant him or her authority to guide and direct our treatment. This authority is not limited to doctors. There are authorities in every field, learned persons who've studied a specific topic, have acquired a beneficial expertise, and consequently have the power to command. To paraphrase Brother David, once people are given power to command, they hang on to that power even beyond their expertise. Then they become authoritarian authorities and keep themselves in that position by putting others down. While genuine authority augments us and builds us up, authoritarian authority puts us down. That is the only way it can retain power.

Brother David then offered a challenging test for leadership and authority: "Does it build others up or does it put them down?"

In the years since I first read Brother David's lecture, I've had many opportunities to assess the quality of one's leadership by that simple test: Are authority and power being used to build someone up or tear someone down?

I recall the sex-abuse scandals in the Roman Catholic Church, the fervent ideology and overreaching power of the George W. Bush administration, the petty tyranny of a school administrator who cared more about his status and power than the children he professed to value. Instance after instance of authoritarianism came to mind. I thought of the church official whose thirst for power and control outweighed nearly every impulse for good, whose uncompromising certitudes made cooperation and moderation seem like vices.

A pastor I knew came under the scrutiny of her authoritarian leader. Her theology was progressive, to the great dismay of her leader who thought it his job to police the pastors in his care and establish theological uniformity. The pastor was summoned before a committee to defend her theology and justify her continued engagement as a minister. To her credit, she stood firm, challenging the motives and legitimacy of the committee that proposed to judge her. In them, she saw power used as a weapon to tear others down. She believed they had lost their credibility, that they had moved from having genuine authority to wielding authoritarian authority, from building others up to tearing others down. As a matter of conscience, she refused to comply with their dictates, affirmed her beliefs, and said she would not recant in order to satisfy a tyrannical minority.

Interestingly, this transpired in a denomination known for its openness to theological exploration. This demonstrates the universality of authoritarianism. Though the areas of disagreement might be different, the compulsion some have to command and control transcends theological climates. An acquaintance once told me that in his very liberal church, where the theological boundaries were so fluid it was nearly impossible to arrive at a consensus on anything, the struggle for power centered on whether the pastor should have an office. Again, those persons bent on power will find any arena in which to assert their dominance.

Sometimes I have wondered if religious institutions, because of their historic emphasis on rules and morality, are especially attractive to persons interested in power and control. A small church I once pastored decided to streamline its outdated and unwieldy committee system by forming one coordinating committee whose members each focused on a specific aspect of the church's life. A church member approached me one Sunday after worship and said if she were not appointed to serve on the committee, she would resign her membership and leave.

More from impulse than careful deliberation, I blurted out, "Why would we appoint you to that role when your commitment to the church is so shallow you would leave if you didn't get your way?" I immediately regretted my comment and tried to temper my remarks, but she was very upset, gathered her things, and left, never to return.

Initially, I felt terribly guilty—there were only twenty members in the church, and I'd caused one of them to leave. I told the elders what I had done and offered to visit her, apologize, and invite her back.

"Please don't," an elder told me. "You have spared our church an immense problem."

I thought his response a bit harsh but soon came to see the wisdom of it. The sooner authoritarianism is challenged, the healthier the church will be. Delaying appropriate challenges to abuses of power only serves to reinforce the validity of the abuser and his or her right to demean others.

Two interesting developments unfolded: Dealing with this woman, and living to tell about it, empowered the congregation to face other issues it had been avoiding, including their tendency to duck unpleasant matters. In the next few months, several difficult decisions were made, the focus of the congregation shifted from inward to outward, and we began to grow. Within a few years, the meetinghouse was full, and a joyous, enthusiastic spirit infused the place.

Several years later, I met the lady who'd left in a huff. We were in a store, walking toward each other. Avoiding contact with her would have been awkward, so I smiled and greeted her, extending my hand to shake hers. She responded by hugging me. I asked about her children, with whom she'd had a rocky relationship while a member of our church, largely because of her efforts to control their early adult lives. She reported that their relationships were mended, that she was now a grandmother, and had experienced some marvelous growth in her life. Though a comment made in haste probably lacked the power to inspire the change I saw in her, I couldn't help but wonder if she'd already been wrestling with issues of power and control and the seed of my remark had fallen on fertile ground.

I wish all such encounters had a positive end. Sometimes those who abuse power lack the self-awareness necessary for transformation. Because religion is attractive to persons interested in control, a vital focus of the church should be the appropriate use of our corporate and individual power toward positive ends. The church should teach us to use power redemptively, to accomplish works of mercy, peace, and reconciliation.

What would the church look like if it valued redemptive peace over authoritarian power?

"What causes wars, and what causes fightings among you? Is it not your passions that are at war in your members? You desire and do not have; so you kill. And you covet and cannot obtain; so you fight and wage war" (James 4:1–2).

I first read those words at the age of eighteen, shortly after the Soviet Union invaded Afghanistan. In response, President Carter ordered young men to register with selective service. Though I had been a Christian all my life, I had become more intentional about my faith and asked the elders in the Quaker meeting I attended to counsel me on this matter. One of them, a delightful woman named Carolyn Kellum, met to speak with me about pacifism. As a result of our conversation, and because I was coming to believe war was inconsistent with the values of Jesus, I chose to register as a conscientious objector. In my naiveté, I believed my Christian friends would affirm my decision, so I was surprised when they not only criticized my pacifism, but suggested war was an appropriate Christian endeavor.

I'm no longer surprised by my fellow Christians' support of war. Indeed, some of the most strident voices for military force emanate from Christian quarters. This, I believe, is the inevitable consequence of an institution that has grown so fond of force and power that it doesn't hesitate to recommend it to others. Additionally, the church has so closely identified itself with the nation that it has lost its prophetic voice and witness, conferring God's blessing to the most immoral undertakings.

It was not always so. For the first several hundred years of the church, Christians believed the ethic of Jesus called them to love and redeem their enemies, not kill them. But what appeared to be a blessing became their undoing. The emperor Constantine was favorably disposed toward Christians, and they now had a stake in his rule and forsook pacifism to perpetuate their position of privilege. So began the uneasy alliance between state and church, which exists to this day, where allegiance to the former almost always compromises the integrity of the latter. To be an American Christian is to hold dual citizenship, forever feeling the tension between the push of country and the pull of discipleship.

The lure of power was an early challenge in the ministry of Jesus. In the fourth chapter of Matthew, Jesus is transported to a high mountain and promised great authority over the world's kingdoms if he will worship Satan. There in a moment is captured the great tension between power and integrity. Lest we think the decision for Jesus was effortless, we need only remember the ordeal left him in need of an angel's care. In the past, when I'd read that famous temptation scene, I tended to marvel at Jesus's willpower, without ever considering the emotional and spiritual energy it took for Jesus to retain his integrity. It was never pointed out that the rejection of such power was so exhausting that Jesus required care.

How much more difficult it must be for us to choose integrity over power.

To be Christian is to hold one's citizenship in an alternative community. "Though we live," as Paul famously stated, "in the world, we are not carrying on a worldly war, for the weapons of our warfare are not worldly but have divine power to destroy strongholds."[3] Such militant language is at first off-putting until we remember the "weapons of our warfare" are peace, humility, kindness, and grace. While these "weapons" might strike us as ineffective, that is only because we have underestimated the world-shifting power of good.

I have a friend who purchased a home in a Southern city. The house had sat empty for some time and was so reasonably priced that my friend feared something was wrong with it. But he could find no defects, so he bought the house and moved in with his wife. Within a few days, he discovered the neighbors on each side of him had been locked in a vicious fight of long duration. The police had been called many times to settle their disputes, their children fought, the men had gone so far as to arm themselves, and each had gotten restraining orders against the other. Each neighbor visited him, trying to enlist my friend on his side. My friend listened carefully, expressed his hope that they would get along, and said that insofar as it depended upon him, he was going to live in peace with all of his neighbors. They each interpreted his refusal to take sides as taking the other's side, and both of them left angry at my friend.

He nevertheless remained kind and took every opportunity to interact with each of them in a positive, loving way. He and his wife invited their children into their home and helped them reconcile their differences. He extended one kindness after another to his neighbors, not taking it personally when they treated him with scorn and disrespect. A year passed with little discernable change, but my friend continued to treat his neighbors with gentle dignity, infusing the area about his home with a spirit, almost an aura, of love. One evening, he looked out his window to see his two neighbors standing in the street, looking on as their children played together. A while later, they shook hands and returned to their homes. Within a few weeks, the restraining orders were forgotten and the families were barbecuing together (a Southern sacrament of reconciliation if ever there were one!).

Had my friend repaid their antagonism with further hostility, the ill will would have escalated and spread. Instead, he recognized the power of peace, patiently extended it to others, and witnessed firsthand the fruit it bore. On the many occasions I've grown impatient or angry with those who've treated me poorly, I remember my friend's steady grace and its power to effect change. It was the power not of an overwhelming force that bludgeoned others into submission but of a persistent love that, as water erodes stone, wore down the hard hate of others.

Early Quakers coined the term "The Lamb's War" to describe the active struggle against evil. The weapons in that effort were the spiritual practices of simplicity, peace, integrity, justice, and equality, empowered by the universal and immanent presence of the living Christ. Thus armed, those early Quakers undertook the transformation of the world about them.

By way of contrast, recall the rise of the Moral Majority in the 1980s, whose lofty endeavors included opposition to the Equal Rights Amendment and the Strategic Arms Limitation Talks. The Religious Right's effective takeover of the Republican Party, their ascendancy to power in the Ronald Reagan and George W. Bush administrations, and their fervent support of military might reveal an infatuation with worldly power and, in the minds of many, a wholesale abandonment of the way of Jesus.

That so many American Christians continue to view military might and power as appropriate tools in the struggle for a transformed world indicates an abject failure to steep ourselves in the alternative worldview of Jesus. The language of reconciliation and redemptive power is a foreign tongue to many in the church.

In the days following the September 11, 2001, attacks on the Twin Towers of the World Trade Center and the Pentagon, a fellow Quaker minister urged his congregation to be mindful of their tradition of peace and not succumb to hate. Within twenty-four hours, he was fired by irate members of his congregation. In the heightened emotion of those days, a gentle reminder to heed our better angels should have been met with appreciation. Instead, the words of peace seemed alien and dangerous, something to be silenced.

That so little of the church's time and effort is spent on a substantive consideration of peace not only reveals the modest value we assign it, but indicates our unease with challenging our culture's love affair with violence and abusive power. Indeed, in some instances it might suggest the church's complicity.

While I don't believe the church has cornered the market on morality, it is called to be a light of peace in a world dark with hate. Churches should, in a very real way, be laboratories of peace, modeling the principles of reconciliation among ourselves, then inviting and equipping the world to do the same. I recall once visiting a church where the pastor droned on about an obscure biblical figure, speculating on his lineage. I glanced around the sanctuary and saw eyes glazed over and people staving off boredom, and I thought, *what a monumental waste of the moment this is.* The church was located in a city beset by violence and poverty. That those entrusted to bring healing and peace were occupying themselves with such inconsequential matters seemed to me reminiscent of those in Jesus's day who tithed mint and dill and cumin but neglected the weightier matters of the law— justice and mercy and faith.

As the church seems to be losing credibility with each new generation, when it glosses over the pressing problems of this world with vague promises of blessings in the next world, an imperative for peace would not only be the world's salvation, but also our own. While the outward forms of this work might differ, the goal would be the same—to teach us how to live in harmony with ourselves, then with our neighbor, and finally with creation and the world.

I know of an inner-city church whose members grew up in the neighborhood, had moved to the suburbs decades before, but returned each Sunday to worship. As the neighborhood around the church changed, the congregation reacted by erecting a fence around their congregants, closing off the one area large enough for neighborhood children to play. No Trespassing signs were posted around the perimeter. A caretaker was hired to watch their grounds and building. Predictably, the church withered, dwindling to a handful of stalwart members, one of whom complained to me, "We can't seem to attract any new people." My observation of the many signs of exclusion fell on deaf ears.

Not three miles away, another church faced a similar challenge. Crime had skyrocketed in their neighborhood as children and teens went unsupervised and unloved. The church responded with a jobs program, employing fifty children to perform service projects during the summer months. Soon the church was overflowing with young people, and the tenor of the neighborhood was transformed as neighbors began to engage one another. Inspired by members of the church, high-school graduates enrolled in college, becoming teachers, lawyers, and nurses, returning to their community to lend a hand-up to others.

To drive past that church building today, one could be forgiven for thinking it was in dire straits—it appears so timeworn and decrepit. But in the places where the true state of the church is measured, in the hearts of its members, it is vital and life giving. At a critical time, it remembered its call to be light and salt and so transformed the world around it. In turn, it raised a new generation of bold thinkers and leaders who will, I have no doubt, be a positive power for mercy and peace. Would that we all could do the same.

1. Joseph Campbell, now deceased, was a mythologist who specialized in the field of comparative religion. He came to my attention after viewing a PBS show by Bill Moyers called "Joseph Campbell and The Power of Myth."
2. I have found the insights of Brother David to be an incalculable help in my own spiritual journey. I urge you to visit his Web site at gratefulness.org.
3. 2 Corinthians 10:3–4.

If the Church Were Christian ...

It Would Care More About
Love and Less About Sex

Many years ago, while still in college, I was invited to pastor a small meeting not far from where I lived. While suspecting we might not see eye to eye on every matter, I believed our differences weren't so great that they couldn't be bridged by the beliefs we held in common. That proved to be the case, and my time there was largely positive.

Several months into my tenure, an elder of the meeting approached me with news that a man and woman in the congregation, both of whom were widowed, had begun living together. The couple, Tom and Maggie, were well into their eighties and had suffered several setbacks, but in their final years they had been fortunate enough to meet and develop a friendship, which eventually blossomed into a deep and mutual affection.

"Did you know they're not married?" the elder asked me. "I think you should talk to them. They're living in sin."

Like many people of my generation, I'd been taught that couples who were romantically involved and living together should be married. It was a principle I'd never questioned, so I agreed with the elder and went to visit them.

Tom and Maggie warmly welcomed me into their modest home, ushered me to their most comfortable chair, and offered me refreshments. It was clear they were honored by my visit and took their responsibility as hosts seriously. Pictures of their respective children and grandchildren lined the walls. I asked their names and received a detailed biography of each family member. They ended by showing me pictures of their deceased spouses.

I seized the opening and commented on their relationship, offering to marry them if they wished.

"We can't afford to," Tom said quietly. "We'd lose too much Social Security. It's all we have." He was obviously embarrassed, and I was starting to feel ashamed for humiliating these kind people.

"We know we shouldn't be living like this," Maggie said, "but a person just gets lonely."

I thought for a moment, then said, "You know, friends, I think God has bigger things to worry about. Let's just be grateful you have each other."

The next Sunday at church, the elder asked if I'd spoken with them. I told him I met with them, explained to him the financial setback they would incur if married, and then suggested he reimburse them their lost income so they could marry. Not surprisingly, he declined my proposal.

Over the next few years, I would watch this elder grow unduly upset whenever someone violated his rather extensive sexual code. He roundly condemned sex outside of marriage, homosexuals, divorce, dancing, or any other activity that he deemed sexual in nature. Indeed, he was so roundly critical of any and all sexual behavior, I began to wonder how he'd fathered his children.

What I didn't realize at the time was the extent to which sexual matters would dominate the church's landscape, particularly as it related to homosexuality. Nor could I imagine the preoccupation, fear, and anger many in the church would exhibit when it came to sexual issues. Many Christians seemed to think sex was the greatest threat to the reign of God, to be endured, not enjoyed, and then only within the narrowest of confines for the purposes of procreation. I often sensed many in the church wished God had devised another method for the continuation of our species.

I suspect this anxiety about sex has its roots in the Victorian mores that influenced early fundamentalism and the apostle Paul's obvious aversion to marriage. In a letter to the church of Corinth, Paul lifted up celibacy as the ideal state, urging people to remain single, to marry only if they lacked self-control or were aflame with passion.[1] Of course, had the church followed Paul's example, there would be no Christians today, just as it is nearly impossible to find a Shaker.[2] Any religion that elevates celibacy as a universal virtue has written its own eulogy. Contrasting Paul's sour assessment of intimacy with the lyrical prose of the Song of Solomon, we begin to see how the formative epistles of the Christian faith cast a shadow on what God intended to be a delight and joy.

After the elder spoke of Tom and Maggie's "living in sin," I began to reflect on their living arrangement. Two lonely persons who'd experienced great loss had the good fortune to find each other. The home they created was one of deep love and mutual respect, a welcome haven to family members and friends. Nothing about any of that felt like sin to me. Indeed, their obvious commitment to each other was so apparent, it mattered little to me that they hadn't participated in a religious ceremony validating their relationship. Watching Tom and Maggie together, especially as they cared for each other in their final years, I believed God consecrated their love far beyond the church's ability to do so.

Several years later, as Maggie lay dying, I stood by her hospital bed with Tom. He held one of her hands; I held the other. For the first time, he told me about his first wife, how she'd been institutionalized for a mental illness, how he'd driven the three hours each way to see her every Saturday, long after she'd forgotten who he was, how he'd raised their children by himself, how his wife had finally passed away.

"I never thought I'd love anyone again," Tom told me. "Then I met Maggie."

They met at the local seniors' center. The next Sunday they went to church together, then out to eat. A year later, they began sharing a home.

"I've loved two good women," Tom told me the day of Maggie's funeral. "I'm a lucky man."

Tom worked most of his life as a laborer. While not a sophisticated man, he knew the value of love. Ironically, the elder who spoke in sanctified tones about love and marriage treated his wife poorly, with scant regard for her feelings and needs. As was the case in the Gospels, the identified "sinner" had a higher commitment to grace than the "saint." We in the church could learn from Tom's example, especially when we gauge the legitimacy of someone's love by his or her compliance to a sexual code that in some instances has outlived its usefulness.

Around that same time, a Quaker organization, the American Friends Service Committee, announced its intention to extend employment to qualified gays and lesbians. This created much anxiety among some Friends in my area, who requested a representative from the AFSC meet with them to hear their concerns. The meeting was held in a private home. I was one of two pastors present, invited at the last moment by the person hosting the meeting. Still new to ministry and a bit naive, I believed the conversation would be candid but civil, so I was taken aback when several persons in attendance demanded that the AFSC rescind its policy, declaring that homosexuals had no place in the church. I was particularly surprised when the other pastor, whom I'd always thought to be a kind and thoughtful man, spoke heatedly against homosexuals. To her credit, the representative patiently explained why they felt it important to not discriminate against persons because of their sexual orientation, reminded us of Quakerism's long history of inclusion, and urged us to study this matter further, predicting (accurately, it turns out) that the issue of homosexuality would one day consume much of the church's attention.

What struck me at the time was not the disparity of views in the room. When I'd first learned of the hiring policy, I knew some persons would oppose it. What surprised me then, and still does, was the intensity with which the discussion was held. The strongest words were directed not toward the AFSC but toward homosexuality itself. It was as if some present were in the grip of a deep fear over which logic and grace had no influence. Homosexuals were accused of "taking over" and "hurting our marriages" and "threatening our children." By the end of the evening, I fully expected them to be blamed for every calamity the world had ever known. The protestor's intense reaction was far out of proportion to the AFSC's decision to hire a gay person and made me realize how uncomfortable and angry many in the church become when asked to expand their understanding of human sexuality.

Within a short time, one of the men present, who'd been most adamantly opposed to the policy, left the church under a cloud of suspicion that he might be gay. When someone condemned his hypocrisy to me, I pointed out that we had given the man little choice, that our hateful treatment of gays made disclosure of his orientation nearly impossible.

Such is the situation we've created in the church—our treatment of those who violate our sexual code is so harsh we discourage honesty. People would rather leave the church than face the criticism and rejection they would experience were the church to discover their private lives. Sadly, this man had invested several years in ministry, served effectively and faithfully, gave every indication of bright promise, but had unfortunately been taught, and believed it himself, that God despised him for his sexual orientation.

The church's preoccupation with sexual "sin" touches those who've ran afoul of its laws through no fault of their own. A woman I know, after marrying the man of her dreams, was devastated to learn he was abusive and controlling. Active in their church, she went to their pastor for counsel, only to be told it was her Christian duty to remain faithful and obedient. After a particularly vicious period of emotional and physical cruelty, she filed for divorce, only to be scorned and rejected by her church, her Christian friends, and her own family, all of whom blamed her for the dissolution of their marriage.

I think of Roman Catholics who've experienced painful divorces then were told by their church they were ineligible to receive the sacrament of holy communion—the central act of Catholic worship. Imagine that! When people are most broken and most in need of the church's ministry of grace, they are judged unworthy to receive what Roman Catholics believe to be the Real Presence of Christ. The church seems so wholly unfamiliar with the gospel tradition of Jesus's reaching out to the hurt and rejected, I can't help but wonder if it is even acquainted with his life and story.

It is as if the church has arrested development and has failed to grow into a healthy understanding of the sexual dimension of life. It is reminiscent of teens who've been told they shouldn't engage in sex, but nevertheless think of it regularly, then are ashamed for an impulse that is natural and human. The horrific abuse of children by priests, the elevation of lifelong celibacy as a spiritual virtue, the all-too-predictable sexual recklessness of prominent evangelicals, and the continued insistence that homosexuals can be "cured," reveal an understanding of sexuality that is both immature and uninformed. The church's failure to develop, model, and articulate a healthy perception of sex confirms the suspicion of many modern people that the church is not a credible witness to the reality of life.

What would it mean if the church cared more about love and less about sex?

To say that the church should care more about love and less about sex is to suggest that the church's preoccupation with sex has had a detrimental effect on the church's well-being. It has so disparaged sexual intimacy that many thoughtful, well-balanced persons want nothing to do with the church, believing it is hopelessly out of touch with what it means to be fully human. By and large, the church has dealt with sexual intimacy by demonizing it or ignoring it. Neither approach is helpful in the church's journey toward wholeness.

An appropriate start toward a healthy sexuality in the church would be a reconsideration of the myths that inform our tradition. One such myth is the Adam and Eve story in which nudity, sin, and shame are closely linked. Prior to their sin of disobedience, Adam and Eve were naked, but "not ashamed."[3] It is only after they have disobeyed God that they are aware of their nudity and shamed by it. The inference is clear—nudity is a source of shame, an indication of human brokenness and failure.

Shortly after the Adam and Eve story, God destroys humanity in a flood, sparing only Noah, his family, and a sampling of animals. It is, in effect, a recreation story, an effort by God to create the world anew. After a rather harrowing boat trip, Noah became drunk, took off his garments, and lay naked in his tent where he was seen by Ham, his youngest son. For this indiscretion, Noah cursed Ham, condemning him and his descendants to slavery. The implications are obvious—while drunkenness and damning your children and grandchildren to slavery are morally acceptable, inadvertently seeing someone nude is not. That Christians condoned slavery for so many centuries, using this story as justification, is yet another sad consequence of bad thinking about human sexuality.

Though Christians have often stigmatized the sexually suspect, there is no evidence Jesus ever did. Instead, he went out of his way to extend grace to such persons, and was often rebuked for his kindness to them. On one occasion, a woman was so profoundly grateful for his mercy, she washed his feet with her tears and anointed him with costly ointment, to the great consternation of his host, whose contempt for the woman was so obvious Jesus could read his thoughts.[4] At the end of the story, it is the broken woman, not the pious man, who is made whole and granted peace.

If early Jewish-Christians had hoped the church might usher in a more enlightened understanding of sexuality, they would be disappointed. Within a relatively short time, Mary, the mother of Jesus, was judged to be a virgin, it being unthinkable that someone of Jesus's stature would have been the result of sexual intercourse. Indeed, so deep was the revulsion toward sex that Mary remained a virgin even after giving birth to Jesus's siblings. Over the years, I've read various explanations of how a virgin might give birth, but each of them required a wholesale suspension of logic. That the church continues to doggedly insist on Mary's virginity as a historic fact not only reveals its unease with sex, it calls into serious question the church's commitment to truth. Its assertion that such claims are a matter of faith, not science, effectively discourages any reasoned analysis and is further evidence of the church's reluctance to honestly examine its foundational beliefs and myths. The church wraps these myths in the cloak of faith, invoking a supernatural privilege, but lives as if these stories have historical merit, continuing to perpetuate the damage caused by unthinking acceptance of stories and legends that even the original writers knew weren't literally true.

It is not likely the church will surrender these myths. But it is possible for the church to place these myths in their proper context, to consider the unintended consequences of their literal acceptance, and to resolve to undo the damage they've caused. Ideally, it might inspire the church to value gracious and mutual love over an archaic sexual code that relegates women to an inferior status. At the very least, the church might no longer let these stories uncritically shape their worldview.

Were the priorities of the church to shift toward love and away from a preoccupation with sexual sin, it might begin to reflect on questions like these: What are the characteristics of gracious and mutual love? Are these qualities confined to marriages? Are these qualities limited to heterosexual relationships? What are the circumstances under which divorce might be appropriate? Does a wedding blessed by the church make a difference in the quality of a marriage? Can people be deeply committed to each other without a religious or legal affirmation of their love? Is sex outside of marriage always wrong? Does God only bless Christian marriage?

Some time ago, I was speaking at an event where I met a man and woman who had been living together nearly twenty years. The year before I met them, they'd begun attending a church but had been asked to leave when it was discovered they weren't married. Ironically, they had wanted to marry years before, but their parents, members of churches that discouraged marriage outside their own denomination, had demanded they break up. The man and woman, then in their late teens, upset with their parents and rejecting the narrow confines of their respective churches, left home and began living together.

"I don't know what we were thinking, going back to church," the man told me. "First, the church told us we couldn't get married. Then it booted us out for not being married. We're damned if we do, and damned if we don't."

I wondered if they'd grown up in fundamentalist sects, and I suggested that if they'd been raised in mainstream churches, that wouldn't have happened.

"I grew up Roman Catholic," the man said, citing the largest Christian denomination in America.

"And I was Baptist," said the woman, citing the second.

The longer we visited, the more I learned about their lives. They were active in their community, spent many hours volunteering to help the poor, seemed bright, inquisitive, and genuinely caring. They were the very sort of people a church would be blessed to have, and because they lived near where I pastored, I invited them to attend our Quaker meeting.

"Thank you, but no," they said. "We're done with the church."

One can't help but wonder what might have happened if they'd come upon a warm, welcoming church the year before. Perhaps the people in that church might have been wrestling with some of the above questions. Perhaps it would have occurred to them that the quality of one's love can't be measured by adherence to an archaic sexual code, and they might have withheld judgment and graciously invited the couple to join their community. Perhaps that couple, as bright and gifted and kind as they were, would have assumed positions of leadership in that congregation and would have equipped that church to expand its ministry of compassion. Perhaps many, many lives would have been bettered because of that couple's decision to participate in a loving community. Perhaps they were the very ones God had called to help bring wholeness to that church. Unfortunately, they flunked the entrance exam.

While those things can't be known, what can be known is that the old morality is no longer holding. If we held on to it because we believed it would enhance our marriages, we were mistaken. Divorce is as common inside the church as outside it. Indeed, a Barna study posted on the religioustolerance.org Web site indicated "divorce rates among conservative Christians were significantly higher than for other faith groups, and much higher than atheists and agnostics experience." George Barna went on to note that upon divorce, many evangelicals experience rejection from their communities of faith rather than care and support.

If Barna's research is accurate, a couple wanting to ensure a lasting marriage should become atheists. But as a person of faith, I'd like to think there is another alternative. That same couple could join a church that values mutual love over slavish obedience to a sexual ethos so rigid even the most scrupulous persons will eventually run afoul of it.[5] That community could help the couple discern what it means to love, could help them embrace a sexuality that is at once gracious, mature, and life enriching, not to mention enjoyable. That community would care less whether the couple were straight or gay and would care more about faithfulness and mutual support. If that couple did divorce, it could help them navigate the territory of grief and loss, assist their growth in self-awareness, and equip them to engage in future relationships more thoughtfully.

The church's failure to deal openly, graciously, and maturely with sexual matters will allow the old patterns of abuse, rejection, sexual discrimination, and homophobia to persist. Sexual intimacy will continue to be a taboo topic; abuse will remain part and parcel of the church experience for some of our women, youth, and children; gay people will continue to be spurned, divorced people will be rejected, and those faithful couples who don't believe a formal church ceremony can make their bond any deeper will continue to be less valued. In the end, the only people comfortable in such a church will be the emotionally and sexually repressed. People searching for fullness of life and joy, for a relevant and reasonable faith, will look elsewhere, probably to those spiritual movements whose worldviews have advanced beyond puberty.

Though not advocating an uncritical acceptance of any and all sexual expressions, I do believe that the mind-set that has long dominated the church, permitting us to casually reject those who fail to meet our standards, is no longer helpful. We are adults, and it is long past time to talk openly and honestly about our needs, desires, and orientations, without fear of shame, ridicule, or rejection. It is, as the apostle Paul so famously declared, time to put away childish ways.

1. 1 Corinthians 7:8–9.
2. After a Civil War peak of five thousand members, there are four Shakers left, all of whom live in Sabbathday Lake, Maine. Celibacy, it turns out, is not especially conducive to community well-being.
3. Genesis 2:25.
4. This story, found in the seventh chapter of Luke, identifies the woman as "a woman of the city, who was a sinner," which was likely New Testament codespeak for a sexual sinner.
5. Remember that the sexual code described in the New Testament (Matthew 5:28–29) holds equally guilty those who desire sexual activity with a woman and those who achieve it. It further advises those who look upon a woman with lust to pluck out their eyes rather than risk the fires of hell.

If the Church Were Christian . . .

This Life Would Be More
Important Than the Afterlife

When I was a child, a man in our hometown had an extensive train set in his basement, where he spent much of his free time. The set was expansive, sprawling across much of the basement, raised several feet off the floor so he could gain access to his Lilliputian world. There were mountains, streets, stores, homes, trees, even a lake, painted blue, with swimmers and boaters and skiers. Around and through the village, over the mountain passes, and beyond the far side of the lake ran a train, threading its way through the tidy landscape.

When word of his train set got out, children began stopping by asking to see it. He would usher us into the basement, a few at a time, and have us watch from a safe distance as he ran the train through its circuit. It was, to my thinking, a world within a world in which he was not only the conductor, but the creator, the mayor, and the master. It was, in every way, a tidy, perfect, manageable world.

His make-believe world supplanted his real one, growing more elaborate and extensive, while the real world deteriorated around him. The paint peeled from his house; weeds grew in the flower beds; the grass went uncut; his wife, family, and friends drifted away. Wars were fought, presidential elections came and went, the world rolled on, but without his participation. Eventually he died, his village was packed up and put away, the effort of his years dismantled in a day, the house sold to another family.

Living as I do in my hometown, I pass by it now and then, remembering the man and his amazing little world beneath the ground. I think of the villages of the mind, the little worlds of our own creation, with their own attendant triumphs and tragedies, and I consider the church and the world it fashioned, one with heroes (Jesus and the saints and us) and villains (Satan and pagans and atheists). Like that man's basement village, the church offered an alternative reality, a place to which one could escape, a neat and ordered world.

I lived in that world a good many years, but the older I grew, the less the church's village satisfied me. Its divorce from reality, its habit of seeing enemies where they were not, its reduction of complex matters to the simplest and starkest terms, and its stubborn insistence that the apex of human understanding was reached some two thousand years ago caused me to question whether a life in the church's world was a life well spent. I was not alone—the exodus of so many thoughtful persons from the church seemed to indicate a widening displeasure with the church's priorities, if not an outright repudiation of the church's worldview.

Additionally, the church's obsession with human destiny, where our souls would reside when they slipped the bonds of earth, seemed to me a minor theme when placed against the wide scope of human suffering. I could no longer believe the arc of God's concern lay principally in whether or not I would go to heaven, when so many others seemed to be living in a present hell.

This preoccupation with the afterlife was prevalent in the churches of my youth. I assumed it was a proper focus of the church's attention and engaged in this emphasis myself, confident this was a task God had set before the church. Then I came to see how the church had used afterlife theology as a bludgeon, wielding it with impunity to bless some and curse others. Always the emphasis was on control—controlling whom God might or might not save, controlling the energies and gifts of others, even controlling what could and could not be thought and taught.

I observed that those persons bent on saving souls and securing a heavenly reward seemed ethically out of balance. They lived in the grip of such fear, they were unable to conduct other aspects of their lives in a healthy and gracious manner. On one occasion, I was meeting with other Quakers discussing homosexuality and whether we would join gays and lesbians in marriage. A woman present blurted out, "We not only shouldn't marry them, we shouldn't let them come to our churches. We're jeopardizing our salvation." Others in the room nodded in agreement, and I began to see how our fears and infatuations with the next life kept us from being gracious in this one.

I remember another time when our yearly meeting[1] had gathered to discuss several difficult issues. As person after person spoke, I began to notice a correlation—those people most obsessed with the afterlife had not lived this life well and wisely. I knew many of these people had strained family relationships, an inability to navigate everyday life, and a diminished capacity for creativity and grace. In focusing on the afterlife, they had neglected to properly engage and nurture this present life. It was as if their emphasis on the next world provided an escape from this world, not unlike the train man and his basement village.

While I caution against an overemphasis on the afterlife, I don't wish to diminish the importance of hope. There are moments when life is so difficult that to long for an afterlife of bliss is understandable. When I was twenty, my closest friend was killed by a drunken driver. The only thought that brought consolation in those first few days was the hope my friend was enjoying the peace and presence of God in a significant way. But as I've grown more familiar with death and dying, my personal need for heaven has diminished. Just as I was not aware of any measure of life prior to my birth, the potential absence of awareness after my death doesn't concern me. It is this life I treasure.

While afterlife imagery can be comforting when life grows difficult, it becomes unhelpful when our dreams and visions of an alternative world so dominate our minds and priorities that we are unable to live well and fully in this world. Matters of injustice and suffering, which should claim our full attention, are dismissed as inconsequential and unimportant, since, in the words of the old gospel tune, "This world is not my home, I'm just apassin' through."

In the first story in the Bible, after God created the world, God gave humans the responsibility of caring for it. Old gospel tunes notwithstanding, this world is our home and our responsibility. To shirk that duty in order to focus on a world we have no verifiable proof even exists is misguided. Yet many Christians still contend that preparing people for an afterlife should be the church's chief priority and willingly commit much energy and money securing entry to heaven even as people suffer and starve for lack of basic necessities.

Not only does our preoccupation with an afterlife cause us to neglect our present lives, it ultimately makes us self-absorbed as the goal of our faith becomes our own eternal well-being. Healthy religion should not consist of saving our skin. I am reminded of the Quaker William Penn, who wrote, "True godliness does not turn men out of the world but enables them to live better in it and excites their endeavors to mend it."[2] Three hundred and fifty years later, too many Christians are content to turn men and women out of the world, and make such a misplaced emphasis seem virtuous.

But what if we heeded Penn's words and found ourselves excited at the prospect of mending the world rather than escaping it? What if we began to take seriously our stewardship of creation? What if our lives weren't something to be passed through or merely endured but were something to be treasured? What if a theology of afterlife no longer dominated our spirituality and we became open to the likely possibility that living our present life well is a sufficient and proper goal?

What if saving the earth were more important than saving our souls?

In my late teens, I became acquainted with an elderly Quaker couple, Ben and Dorotha, who attended the same meeting as I and lived in an old farmhouse at the edge of town. Their manner of living was very simple, and without knowing much about them, I assumed they were people of modest means. They dressed very simply, drove a well-used car, and gave every outward appearance of having a limited income. In fact, they owned a significant amount of land in a quickly developing area and had many assets at their disposal. I was a guest in their home several times and began to understand

some of the themes that ordered their lives: simplicity, generosity, thoughtful stewardship of their resources, and a desire
to live joyfully and freely, unburdened by the demands of
material possessions.

Ben and Dorotha were doing this with such grace and
cheer that I was inspired to befriend them. As I got to know
them, I learned their simplicity wasn't motivated by a mi-
serly, stingy spirit. Their interest was not in spending as little
money as they could in order to accumulate more. Their
desire was to live so lightly upon the land that others could
also benefit from their resources. To that end, they lived on
one Social Security check and gave the other away. They
raised chickens so they could distribute eggs. They had extensive gardens and shared their produce. They opened their
home to guests and persons in need. They embodied, in every
way, the principle of mutual care and responsibility.

I had encountered many kind people before, but their
compassion was often sporadic and impulsive, inspired by a
person or situation that had caught their attention. Consequently, their generosity usually required little of them—no
change of lifestyle, no altering of their priorities or desires,
and no self-examination of their living patterns. What intrigued me about this elderly couple was the deliberation
with which they lived. Not content to give sporadically as they
were inspired, Ben and Dorotha seemed intentional about
their manner of living and its implications for the wider
world. Consequently, they lived far beneath their means and

put their assets to good use for others, serving as the genesis of many worthwhile endeavors in our community.

But their contributions went far beyond financial generosity. They befriended the forgotten and marginalized, visited nursing homes, cared for the poor, were present for sick and lonely people, even visited schools to encourage and help children. Dorotha played the violin, not with a high degree of skill, but with an infectious enjoyment. She would take it along on her appointed rounds, providing impromptu concerts. This came to symbolize the theme of her life—wherever she went, one could expect music and life and joy.

Though deeply involved in the life of their Quaker meeting, theirs was not a faith that required propagation. Indeed, they seemed uneasy when conversation turned toward religion or theology and would usually excuse themselves to go do something useful. Ben and Dorotha sought no converts and held no creed except that of doing good. As for power, they did nothing to gain it or seek it out but lived with such integrity that others regularly looked to them for guidance. Their power was earned by wisdom, not conferred by position, and they wielded it lightly.

On the occasion of their deaths, family and friends gathered to remember their contributions. Concurrently, I had been reflecting upon the nature of religious leadership in various cultures. Sociology has long been an interest of mine, especially the role of religion in society. As I listened to people speak about these two wonderful people, I thought of the roles they'd played in our Quaker meeting and community and was struck by the similarities between their lives and the lives of those I'd lately been reading about.

In every culture there are persons who fill the position of community elders. These are men and women whose wisdom, generosity of spirit, wide concern, and inclusive love equip them to care for people beyond their kith and kin. Their goal is not just the well-being of their family and friends; they want the global community to prosper and do well. Ideally, our religious communities should be full of such people, inspiring and equipping others to expand their worldview. Instead, religion has too often narrowed our affections and dampened our global concerns.

Encountering Ben and Dorotha in the dawn of my spiritual life was providential. At the same time, I was working alongside Christians who viewed humanity as inherently corrupt and fallen, who had little concern for those beyond their faith, and who had a stunted imagination for what the world could be and little desire to change it. To have those two visions so clearly presented at a formative stage in my faith enabled me to better discern the scope and focus of my own life and ministry. I decided not to invest any effort in saving people's souls from a hell I didn't believe in. Rather, I would work to expand my understanding of God, deepen my commitment to grace, and uplift the human condition.

I also resolved that even if my search for truth and commitment to grace led me away from God and the church,

I would still pursue those virtues, believing they were the highest ideals, worthy of my attention and devotion. I would eventually stop believing in God. More accurately, I stopped believing in the God of my youth, whose sole interest seemed to be saving us from hell. While I've not yet arrived at a definitive understanding of God and don't suspect I ever will, I believe any god unconcerned with this life merits neither our attention nor devotion. For if God can so easily dismiss this life and world, so, too, will God's people, and our indifference will eventually be seen as saintly.

As a consequence of my growing interest in practical spirituality, I began noticing people who worked creatively to bring heaven to earth. One August in the early 1990s, I attended our yearly meeting sessions where I met a man named Roland Kreager, who was working for an organization called the Right Sharing of World Resources. Its goal was to encourage more affluent persons to provide loans and grants to the less fortunate, enabling them to begin local businesses and employ their peers. Roland spoke about entire villages transformed when cottage industries, financed by the Right Sharing of World Resources, extended employment to the desperately poor. In the following years, I would learn more about Roland and the work of Right Sharing throughout Africa and Asia. Today, over sixty projects contribute to the peace, daily sustenance, medical care, and education of thousands of people. This is done simply, and without fanfare, bringing hope and help to the destitute and forlorn.

Not long after meeting Roland, I was invited to speak at a large gathering. Troubled by Christianity's historic emphasis on saving souls in foreign lands, I thought the people of Africa would benefit more from potable water, medicine, stable government, and sustainable agriculture than they would from hearing a man warn them of a hell they knew all too well. I spoke plainly about the need for a shift in our concerns.

Afterward, a woman took me to task for questioning the church's priorities. She and her church were in the process of raising tens of thousands of dollars to send a missionary to Africa. I urged her and her church to send mosquito nets instead, under which the African children could sleep and be protected from malaria-bearing mosquitoes. This was not said in a flippant manner. I was quite serious and simply suggesting an alternative to soul saving I believed would be more beneficial and practical.

She responded by saying my comments were an insult to all Christians everywhere.

Isn't it odd? Christians created a theological scenario that placed the soul of every person at risk of eternal damnation. To counter that threat, we interpreted the life and death of Jesus in a particular way, then spent billions of dollars battling the very threat we created. Wouldn't it just be easier to stop perpetuating the scenario?

Perhaps the day might come when Christianity will reconsider its priorities, when preparing souls for an afterlife we have no proof exists fades in importance, and we can use the church's energies to improve this life. I have caught glimpses of what that might look like in the quiet, daily work of Ben and Dorotha and the useful efforts of Roland Kreager. As I've visited churches around the country, I've found others engaged in similar work, though seldom enough persons as need requires. While there is always an abundance of people willing to create and enforce orthodoxy, while fortunes are spent saving people from the imaginary dangers of imaginary places, only a relative few take up the god life Penn described, which doesn't "turn men out of the world but enables them to live better in it and excites their endeavors to mend it."

If the church were Christian, we would do what Jesus did—equip one another to live better in this world and stop fretting about the next one. To study the Gospels is to encounter a man who cared deeply about this life. His passion for justice, mercy, and grace shone through his words and works. An immediacy, a sense of urgency, marked his movement. This was not a man bent on winning souls for some far-off heaven on some distant day. When his disciples asked him how to pray, he told them to pray that God's kingdom would come to earth. Now was the day of salvation. And what was that salvation? It was the day when all of humanity would be so imbued with God's presence that we would hunger and thirst for righteousness. Salvation would be when heaven was in us, not when we were in heaven. It would happen when we stopped worrying about saving our own skin and cared more about saving and restoring the land and sea and sky and all who dwell therein.

1. A yearly meeting is the Quaker equivalent of a diocese. It is comprised of any number of Quaker meetings, usually in the same geographic area, who unite together to accomplish a larger mission or task.
2. This and other Quaker insights can be found in the *Quaker Faith and Practice* of Britain Yearly Meeting (1995 edition).

A Closing Word

Quite a few years ago, I was given a copy of the book *Zen and the Art of Motorcycle Maintenance* by a friend who knew I rode motorcycles, believed the book was a repair manual, and thought it might it helpful. The author of the book, Robert Pirsig, used a motorcycle trip as the setting to talk about relationships and values. In that book he told about a clever method used in southern India to capture monkeys. A hole is drilled into a coconut, then the insides are hollowed out and filled with rice. The coconut is then chained to a stake driven in the ground.

The hole is just large enough for a monkey to insert its paw but too small for it to remove its paw once it is filled with rice. The monkey, unwilling to let go of the rice, is effectively trapped. It needs only to let go of the rice to gain its freedom but doesn't understand that, so it remains ensnared, ironically, by the very thing it believed would sustain its life.

I reread the book not long ago and was struck by the broader implications of that illustration. The church, it seems to me, is now captured by the very things it believed would nourish it. The inevitable accumulation of myths, creeds, traditions, and structures (both physical and institutional) have rendered the church immovable. Just when the church needs most to be nimble, it is inflexible, holding fast to customs and beliefs that more and more people are finding unhelpful and unintelligible. Is it any wonder that while an increasing number of people are defining themselves as spiritual, fewer and fewer of them look to the church as a community that can assist their journey? It is time the church "let go of the rice."

Unfortunately, when change does come to the church, it is almost always superficial, akin to painting a steam locomotive a new color and hailing it as a revolution in transportation. A new church building was recently constructed several miles from my home. As it was being built, signs were displayed announcing it would be a church like nothing ever before experienced, a new way of being the church. Advertisements began running in the newspaper, targeting people who'd left organized religion, inviting them to return. When the church finally opened its door, I attended, intrigued by their claim of "a new way of being the church." While there, I discovered their promise was overstated. Though the songs were new, the message was one I'd heard countless times before. It had simply been repackaged to suit a contemporary audience.

When one considers the many reformations in the church over the centuries, one gets the feeling they were efforts to re-brand the church, more a marketing ploy and less a dramatic transformation.

While people have predicted the demise of the church ever since its inception, I don't believe the church will die altogether. There will always be persons who find meaning in the religious dimension of life, even as others will find religion meaningless. Even in my lifetime, atheism has lost its stigma. One day, sooner than later, politicians will not have to adopt the guise of piety in order to gain elective office. Ironi-cally, even as religion will lose its cultural significance, more and more people will yearn for a spiritual dimension to their lives. They simply won't look to the church to provide it.

While speaking at the Plymouth Congregational Church in Wichita, Kansas, I met Don Olsen, who serves that church as the senior minister. In a dinner conversation, Don said, "I believe the church of the future will be an institution for rites of passage."

I asked him what he meant by that, and he explained that in Europe the church had become the place people went to be married, have their children baptized, and their funer-als held. Its role in European society was largely symbolic; people no longer looked to the church as a faith community to which they could commit their spiritual lives. Interest-ingly, even as the church's influence in Europe has waned, the nations of Europe have adopted many of the church's priorities—gracious assistance is provided to the poor, the ill have access to quality health care regardless of their ability to pay, and laws protect religious and ethnic minorities. It is as if the church accomplished what it had set out to do—helped create a system of governance that embraced the priorities of Jesus—and now existed chiefly to celebrate and affirm significant life moments. In essence, the church worked itself out of a job. Perhaps this is the inevitable evolution of all nations where Christianity was, or is, the formative faith, and might well predict the future of Christian faith in America.

If there is a future for the church in America, perhaps it is to raise America's collective consciousness, so that injustice, poverty, and tyranny would be moral affronts to us and we would hasten to eliminate them. Such a church would creatively and consistently call us to heed our better angels. It would actively engage our leaders, urge gracious treatment for the poor and powerless, promote peace and reconciliation among nations, challenge abusive religion, and provide a setting where people could reflect upon significant matters. The central task of this church would not be convincing us to believe doctrines about Jesus. Rather, it would help us live out the priorities of Jesus—human dignity, spiritual growth, moral evolution, and the ongoing search for truth and meaning.

Its task would not be to confer God's blessing upon the American way of life, but to help us transcend the parochialism that grips so many of us. That such a church is needed is clearly evident. As I write this, in the middle months of 2009, America is engaged in two wars, is suffering the economic consequences of unchecked greed, and is witnessing the rapid erosion of the middle class as more of our citizens slip into poverty. If it has not always been so, it is now obvious our nation needs spiritual communities that appropriately challenge the assumption that God has mandated our style and standard of living. Whether the same church that has walked hand in hand with the powers and principalities can now become a light unto the nation isn't known, but if it does, it will have to radically change its role and purpose. For the world can no longer afford a myopic church, closely allied with any one nation or class. It will have to "let go of the rice," surrendering the priorities and principles it once believed essential to its life. Perhaps this is what Jesus meant when he spoke of losing our lives to save them.

Discussion Questions

Chapter 1: Jesus Would Be a Model for Living Rather Than an Object of Worship

1. It is not unusual for religions to deify (to make a god of or take as an object of worship) religious leaders, prophets, or founders. Why do you suppose religions do that? What practical purpose does that serve? How might it be unhelpful?

2. How central is the moral perfection of Jesus to your faith? Why is that important or unimportant to you?

3. How would you live differently if Jesus were a model of living, not an object of worship?

Chapter 2: Affirming Our Potential Would Be More Important Than Condemning Our Brokenness

1. Can you remember the first time a religious leader or parent said you were a sinner? Did you believe him or her? What effect has that had on your relationship with God? With others?

2. While I speak of the negative effects of guilt, is there such a thing as "good" guilt?

3. What does it mean to be created in the image of God?

Chapter 3: Reconciliation Would Be Valued over Judgment

1. This chapter begins with a memory of the rite of confession. Do you think such a rite could be helpful in your spiritual journey? Why or why not?

2. Are you estranged from someone you were once close to? What would need to happen for reconciliation to occur?

3. Do you think it might be helpful for the church to have a rite of divorce as described in this chapter? Why or why not?

Chapter 4: Gracious Behavior Would Be More Important Than Right Belief

1. If being Christian means believing the right things about Jesus, who decides what those right things are?

2. Would a gracious atheist be welcomed in your church?

3. What is the correlation between playfulness and rigid religion?

Chapter 5: Inviting Questions Would Be Valued More Than Supplying Answers

1. If you could ask any question of the church, what would it be? How does it feel to ask that question?
2. Could your search for truth ever lead you away from the church?
3. Describe a church that values questions as much as it values answers.

Chapter 6: Encouraging Personal Exploration Would Be More Important Than Communal Reform

1. If you belong to a church, are you expected to believe certain things? Are there patterns of behavior you are expected to follow to be accepted? How did these expectations arise? Who decided and enforced them?
2. Have you ever felt shunned? Have you ever shunned?
3. What would a church look like that valued personal exploration over communal uniformity?

Chapter 7: Meeting Needs Would Be More Important Than Maintaining Institutions

1. Do you agree with Will Campbell, that "all institutions, every last single one of them, are evil; self-serving, self-preserving, self-loving, and very early in the life of any institution it will exist for its own self"?

2. Can you think of an institution that has remained true to the vision that gave it birth?

3. Does working with others in the church to meet human need restore your love for the Christian community?

Chapter 8: Peace Would Be More Important Than Power

1. Can you explain the difference between authority and authoritarianism? Why does the first often lead to the second?

2. If, as some claim, America is a Christian nation, does that justify Christian participation in war?

3. Do you believe the church is attractive to persons seeking power and control? If so, why is that?

Chapter 9: It Would Care More About Love and Less About Sex

1. Do you believe the church, generally speaking, has a healthy understanding of human sexuality?

2. Has the church's understanding of sexuality caused it to be less gracious to people who don't meet the church's expectations?

3. What do you believe should be the standards for Christian marriage?

Chapter 10: This Life Would Be More Important Than the Afterlife

1. Is the church's historic emphasis on the afterlife a proper concern for the church?
2. How would the church be different if its primary concern were proper stewardship of this life and world?
3. Can you think of your own "Ben and Dorotha," persons who seemed to have a deep sense of community and caring?

A Concluding Question

I have emphasized ten aspects of the church I believe should change if the church were to take seriously the ethic of Jesus. Can you think of any others?

READ AN EXCERPT FROM
PHILIP GULLEY'S NEW BOOK

~

The Evolution of Faith

How God Is Creating a
Better Christianity

One

The Evolution of Faith

Several years ago at the invitation of a friend, I attended his childhood church on the Sunday it celebrated its one hundredth anniversary. The pastor, in an exuberant moment, spoke of the enduring proclamation of the church, how since the time of Jesus the unchanging Christian gospel had been proclaimed throughout the world. The congregation nodded in agreement, even affirming its assent with robust *Amens*. As a student of church history, I knew the pastor's claims were inaccurate. I knew that over the past two thousand years, the church's message had experienced significant change, influenced by pivotal figures and movements. I even suspected that specific church had experienced considerable theological change over its hundred years, reflecting the varied perspectives of its leaders.

I thought of the diverse mutations of Christianity I had encountered in my life—the Roman Catholicism of my mother, the Baptist leanings of my father's family, the Church of Christ tradition of a brother and sister, the Methodist perspective of another brother, the Presbyterian community of yet another sibling, and my own Quaker tradition. Each of these expressions emphasized a particular facet of the Christian experience. Each understood the mission of the church differently, employed different styles of worship. They did not agree on how God's will was known, and were not in harmony about the priorities of Jesus. They did not share a common understanding of what it meant to be Christian, what it meant to please God, or how the church should be governed. Though they all bore the Christian name, their differences in belief were so considerable one could reasonably conclude they practiced different religions altogether. And that was just Christianity in the Western world. Were we to have stirred into the mix the many strains of Eastern Orthodoxy, the differences would be staggering indeed.

Though I disagreed with the pastor's claim of an unchanged church, I understood his motives for making such an assertion. The church's authority rests on its declaration of doctrinal purity, and her ageless, unchanging truths. Pastors who acknowledge the church's changing truth must convince congregants he or she nevertheless speaks with authority—a hard enough task in a culture already suspicious of institutional power.

At first glance, the title of this book, *The Evolution of Faith: How God is Creating a Better Christianity,* seems presumptuous and egotistical, as if God is using me to liberate Christianity from its ancient moorings and carry it forward. But on closer examination, it makes perfect sense. If there are many versions of Christianity, and if Christianity has mutated and evolved over the centuries, it's reasonable to conclude it will continue to do so. It also is reasonable to conclude God might inspire a number of people to shepherd that process, and that I might be one of them—just as you might be—and a fitting response is to share our insights with others. Therefore, to speak of an evolving Christianity isn't to undertake a radical and unilateral overhaul of Christianity, but to suggest a possible way forward that not only honors the ethos of Jesus but is conversant with our time and culture. For while it is clear that Christianity has and will change, what is less clear are the forms it might take.

What are the cultural factors that make an evolving Christianity inevitable? At the Quaker meeting I pastor, a woman of the Baha'i faith joins her Quaker husband in meeting for worship. Another attendee, a Jewish man, teaches an adult Sunday school class. A young man in the congregation met a woman of the Muslim faith while in college, they married, and are warmly welcomed into our meeting. Another man, intelligent and deeply caring, speaks openly about his leanings toward atheism. Imagine my standing at the pulpit and pronouncing these people spiritually lost, urging them to accept Jesus as their Savior. Not only would my sense of decorum prohibit that, so would my appreciation for their obvious virtues. They are, to a person, loving, gracious, and wise. For me to suggest they were spiritually inferior would not only be unkind, it would be untrue.

At one time, I thought such diversity was rare, but as I speak with my colleagues in ministry, I've discerned it is not at all unusual. More and more people are marrying outside their childhood faith, couples are finding joy and meaning in other spiritual expressions, and many churches are incorporating these persons into their fellowships with sensitivity and warmth. This widespread openness to diverse religious traditions points to an evolving Christianity more tolerant than its predecessors.

In addition to this spiritual diversity, the pervasive acceptance of scientific advancements has significantly altered Christianity, especially those kinds of Christianity predicated on an outdated worldview. It is no longer possible for people to reject the scientific evidence of creation without seeming ignorant. Nor is it possible, given what we know about homosexuality, to sustain a Christianity that asserts one's sexual orientation is chosen or inherently sinful. Add to this the stunning social changes brought about by the Internet, making spiritual and cultural isolation nearly impossible. Narrow religions can only be sustained when and where information is limited and controlled, when people are able to be "not of the world." But the Internet has dramatically shrunk our world, making isolation from divergent views nearly impossible.

Case in point: At the urging of my publisher, I began a Facebook page. I have several thousand Facebook friends from a variety of geographical and religious backgrounds. Nearly every week, I post a theological or spiritual question, inviting responses. Given the diversity of my friends, the answers differ widely. I expected this. What I did not expect was the extent to which my Facebook friends would engage one another. Almost without exception, those exchanges have been cordial and sincere, with persons expressing much interest in the views of others, saying such things as, "I see your point. It makes a lot of sense. I'll have to rethink this."

The church's monopoly on Christian instruction is over. People feel quite free to join in theological discourse without the buffer of the church or its clergy. Were I in a religious tradition that emphasized the supremacy of a professional religious hierarchy, I would worry for my job, for it is apparent more and more people are looking to other spiritual resources beyond the conventional ones offered by the church. Whether people turn to a Facebook friend, or a TV talk show, a neighbor, or a best-selling book, they are seeking religious counsel and spiritual insight outside the church. As they do, the church's authority—already weakened by scandal, abuse, and irrelevancy—will evaporate altogether.

These cultural factors—religious diversity, advancements in science, expanded communication, and the church's diminishing role as the sole religious authority—are making the next stage of Christianity not only possible, but inevitable. Ironically, the more the church resists this evolution, the more likely it will hasten the change, for its efforts to preserve the status quo will only emphasize its more negative attributes of rigidity, control, and fear, thereby alienating the very people it wishes to influence.

An Evolving Christianity Requires An Emerging Theology

There has never been a significant shift in the church's structure that wasn't accompanied by or inspired by a theological change. When Martin Luther initiated the Protestant Reformation, he jettisoned many elements of the prevailing theology, including the means of salvation, the authority of the pope, and the necessity of priestly intervention for the forgiveness of sins. Whether a changing church is inspired by an emerging theology, or a new theology materializes as a consequence of changes in the church, one is never seen without the other. For change in the church never happens unless we also have convinced ourselves God prefers that change, and as a result, have constructed a theology that justifies the changes we've made.

I am no different. In my case, my experience of the

Divine Presence called into question many of the church's practices, particularly the issues of institutional governance, doctrinal authority, the scope of salvation, and the power of grace. I have spent a good deal of my adult life constructing a theology that rationally supports the spiritual values I first embraced from instinct. Some Christians have reacted strongly to this, accusing me of heresy. What they fail to realize is how their own views—now considered traditional and orthodox—were at one time deemed revolutionary, if not heretical. One hundred years ago, their Christianity was the new Christianity.

A Preview of a Future Christianity

The theology in which many of us were raised fits hand in glove with the prevailing understanding of the church. It was exclusive, rarely acknowledging the merits of other religions. It emphasized a God above and beyond us, mirroring the ecclesial structure of the day that elevated leadership and concentrated power in the hands of an exalted few. It was decidedly privileged in nature and view, reflecting the cultural mores of the richest nations. Its God took their side, blessed their priorities, and helped secure their wealth and status. When Leonardo Boff, a Brazilian priest, criticized the church's alliance with the wealthy and powerful, he was accused of Marxism and silenced by the Roman Catholic's

Congregation for the Doctrine of the Faith, led by Cardinal Joseph Ratzinger, who later would become Pope Benedict XVI. Under pressure from the Vatican, Boff eventually surrendered his priestly orders. This was all too common in a Christianity of dominance and control, but will not stand in the emerging Christianity, whose philosophy will focus less on power and self-preservation and more on ecclesial modesty and service. Perhaps the evolved Christianity will ironically go back as it moves forward. Perhaps it will more accurately reflect the servant spirit of Jesus of Nazareth, and be less concerned with worshipping Christ the King. For where the primary focus of a spiritual community is the worship of its central figure, the patterns of hierarchy become established, formalized, and perpetuated, eventually demanding unthinking conformity and unquestioning obedience.

My hope is that an evolving Christianity will reflect the egalitarian spirit of Jesus, not the elitism of an entrenched church. It will no longer presume that male genitalia uniquely equips someone for leadership. Nor will it assume heterosexuals are capable of ministry in a way homosexuals are not. It will listen carefully to its young people, letting their enthusiasm and yearning for authenticity inspire a passionate and relevant faith. It will console the brokenhearted, speak for the voiceless, befriend the weak, challenge the powerful, and call to leadership those who handle power well—not for selfish gain but for selfless service.

An evolved Christianity will not insist we believe the absurd, affirm the incredible, or support a theology that degrades humanity. It will be a friend of science, working joyfully alongside the best minds in the world on a common mission to embrace and enhance life. This Christianity will talk less and act more. I recently attended a church gathering in which a committee had been asked to draft a resolution against torture. They had spent an entire year writing a short paragraph on which everyone on the committee could finally agree, but no one else would likely read. When a woman rose to suggest they actually do something to prevent torture, rather than just write words against it, she was criticized for not cooperating. People no longer listen to the church's pronouncements. No one waits with baited breath for the church to wade in with its perspective. We craft missives, epistles, and minutes that are first ignored, then forgotten. Nor do governments change their policies because Christians have collected on a street corner to sing "We Shall Overcome." But when ministers are bold and prophetic, when Christians rise from their pews and work and sweat and invest their lives, people take notice and lives are changed.

The richness of an evolved Christianity won't lie in slavish obedience to antiquated claims, but rather in a vigorous commitment to care for the marginalized and in an honest search for meaning and truth, no matter where that search might lead. It is exciting beyond words to stand on the threshold of such a movement, to watch it unfold and flower, to watch it not only restore the church—which it just might, though that is not its purpose—but refresh and restore our world.

In the chapters ahead, I'll use as my framework the traditional areas of concern for Christian theology. Though that conventional structure is still an appropriate one, it is long past time its assertions were reexamined and reinterpreted in light of our changing world and expanding consciousness. Perhaps you have not been accustomed to viewing faith from the vantage point of these topics, believing such matters are best left to theologians. But I believe these subjects have a tremendous influence on our personal spiritual journeys, helping us to negotiate and navigate a more meaningful life. Just as the prophet Ezekiel saw a valley of dry bones stirring to life, so too can new life be breathed into our moribund faith, and God might say to us, as God said to them, "I will put my Spirit in you and you will live." (Ezekiel 37:14, NV)

In the past ten years, Phil has enjoyed speaking at conventions, colleges, libraries, and churches around the country. For a list of his upcoming appearances, or to schedule him for your event or organization, please visit www.PhilipGulley.org and click on the Events button.

Phil continues to pastor at Fairfield Friends Meeting near Indianapolis. You may download his weekly messages at www.PhilipGulley.org. Click on the GraceTalk button and enjoy! For directions to Fairfield Friends Meeting, visit www.fairfieldfriends.org.

To learn about Phil's other nonfiction, the Porch Talk series, visit www.philipgulleybooks.com.

To discover Phil's wonderful fictional world of Harmony, Indiana, visit www.harmonyseries.com.

Because of the volume of mail he receives, Phil is unable to respond to every written letter. But if you e-mail him at Phil@PhilipGulley.org, he'll respond in a timely manner.

Thank you.